ARGENTINA

GOOD STORIES REVEAL as much, or more, about a locale as any map or guidebook. Whereabouts Press is dedicated to publishing books that will enlighten a traveler to the soul of a place. By bringing a country's stories to the English-speaking reader, we hope to convey its culture through literature. Books from Whereabouts Press are essential companions for the curious traveler, and for the person who appreciates how fine writing enhances one's experiences in the world.

"Coming newly into Spanish, I lacked two essentials—a childhood in the language, which I could never acquire, and a sense of its literature, which I could."

—Alastair Reid, *Whereabouts: Notes on Being a Foreigner*

OTHER TRAVELER'S LITERARY COMPANIONS

<table>
<tr><td>*Amsterdam*</td><td>*Ireland*</td></tr>
<tr><td>*Australia*</td><td>*Israel*</td></tr>
<tr><td>*Brazil*</td><td>*Italy*</td></tr>
<tr><td>*Chile*</td><td>*Japan*</td></tr>
<tr><td>*China*</td><td>*Mexico*</td></tr>
<tr><td>*Costa Rica*</td><td>*Prague*</td></tr>
<tr><td>*Cuba*</td><td>*South Africa*</td></tr>
<tr><td>*France*</td><td>*Spain*</td></tr>
<tr><td>*Greece*</td><td>*Vienna*</td></tr>
<tr><td>*India*</td><td>*Vietnam*</td></tr>
</table>

ARGENTINA

A TRAVELER'S LITERARY COMPANION

EDITED BY
JILL GIBIAN

WHEREABOUTS PRESS
BERKELEY, CALIFORNIA

Published by
Whereabouts Press
Berkeley, California
www.whereaboutspress.com

Distributed to the trade by PGW / Perseus Distribution

MANUFACTURED IN THE UNITED STATES OF AMERICA

Library of Congress Cataloging-in-Publication Data
Argentina : a traveler's literary companion /
edited by Jill Gibian.
p.   cm. —
(Traveler's literary companions ; 17)
A collection of short fiction by the best writers
of Argentina, arranged geographically.
ISBN 978-1-883513-19-1 (alk. paper)
1. Argentina—Fiction.
2. Short stories, Argentine—Translations into English.
I. Gibian, Jill.
PQ7777.E5A74   2010
863'.0108982—dc22
2010039782

5 4 3 2 1

Contents

BUENOS AIRES

CAPITAL CITY AND PROVINCE

THE WESTERN REGION

EL CUYO TO THE ANDES
MENDOZA, SAN JUAN, SAN LUIS, LA RIOJA

THE SOUTHERN REGION

PATAGONIA TO TIERRA DEL FUEGO
NEUQUÉN, RÍO NEGRO, SANTA CRUZ

Preface

When I think of going anywhere, I think of going
south. I associate the word "south" with freedom.
——PAUL THEROUX, *Nowhere Is a Place:*
Travels in Patagonia

The motif of the south carries a myriad of connotations
within the Latin American experience. In the context of
Argentina, the south for some extends only as far as Buenos Aires, that city of eternal light whose iconic *Obelisco*
along the sixteen-lane Avenida 9 de Julio, bears witness
to the many facets of urban reality. For the more literal
minded, the south extends beyond the Pampas and the
Patagonia to Tierra del Fuego—a south once populated
by indigenous cultures such as the Tehuelche, literally the "people of the south," who were reputed to be
giants according to Antonio Pigafetta's 1520 account of
Magellan's voyage. And yet for the many who were forced
into exile during the years of the dictatorship, the south
denotes *retorno*, the return to homeland.

Vuelvo al Sur
como se vuelve siempre al amor.
I return to the South like one always returns to love.

Argentina: A Traveler's Literary Companion joins an
exciting series whose aim is to invite travelers to experi-

ence a country through its literature, whether they travel in the conventional sense or from the comfort of an armchair. To this end, the anthology is organized into geographic regions: The Northern Region (El Gran Chaco), the Central Region (El Litoral), Buenos Aires (capital city and province), the Western Region (the Andes), and the Southern Region (Patagonia to Tierra del Fuego). The vastness of Argentina rings clear through these stories, and the urban stands in sharp contrast with the rural. The anthology also makes a quick foray into Uruguay in the section entitled Beyond the River Plate.

The geography of the north is poignantly portrayed through Héctor Tizón's story, "Old Horse," as we watch the old horse traverse the rugged landscape for the last time. Set in El Litoral in central Argentina, Adolfo Bioy-Casares's story "About the Shape of the World" leads us up river to Uruguay through the confluences of the River Plate, and the Uruguay and Paraná Rivers on a mystical journey that is at once surreal and sensual. Carlos Chernov's story "The Tourist" has us climbing Aconcagua, the tallest mountain in the Western Hemisphere, on a decisive ascent toward destiny. Down south in the Patagonia, we find remnants of native cultures, ostrich-like rheas known as *ñandúes* and characters like Borges' Juan Dahlman, for whom the South offered a romantic escape into the past, a past where gauchos still ruled, and dying in a knife fight was far more honorable than being saved by modern alternatives.

Llevo el Sur,
como un destino del corazón.
I carry the South like a destiny of my heart.

In Buenos Aires Marcelo Birmajer's "The Last Happy Family" introduces us to the Jewish community of Barrio Once, Alicia Steimberg's narrator is wary of "The Man with Blue Eyes," Edgar Brau's "The Blessing" has us dodging bullets outside the Pink House (Argentina's equivalent to our White House), Ana María Shua tells us a tender "Bed Time Story," and José Eduardo Totah reminds us of the importance of *fútbol,* Argentina's national pastime. The tango is tacity celebrated in Julio Cortázar's "Return Trip Tango" by bringing us a romantic intrigue that echoes the themes of early tangos, and Luisa Valenzuela's "The Place of Its Solitude" posits urban against rural in a story that foreshadows the tragic events of Argentina's Dirty War (1976–1983) during which some 30,000 people were disappeared.

Soy del Sur,
como los aires del bandoneón.

I am from the South, like the sounds of the bandoneón.

This volume consists of eighteen stories. That number could easily have been multiplied many hundreds of times over. To narrow the wealth of the Argentine narrative to such a finite number automatically begs the readers' forgiveness. Even before Borges paved the way in the mid-20th century for the writers of the Latin American Boom—whose innovations in narrative structure and use of magic realism and the fantastic were to revolutionize Latin American literature forever—Argentina had established itself as having one of the richest literary traditions in all of Latin America. In fact, Argentina is credited with the first Latin American short story, "El matadero"

("The Slaughterhouse"), written by Esteban Echeverría
in 1839 while living in exile in Uruguay and published
posthumously in 1871 after the overthrow of Juan Manuel
de Rosas.

Literary production in Argentina began to soar in the
first part of the 20th century thanks in part to a number
of literary journals such as *Proa* and *Martin Fierro*. While
both journals continued to publish foreign literature, the
focus gradually shifted to the River Plate. The *martin-
fierristas*, in particular, were concerned with exploring
questions of national identity: What did it mean to be
Argentine? Is there a unique Argentine sensibility? In
1931, the literary journal *Sur* was founded by Victoria
Ocampo with a list of distinguished collaborators that
included Borges, Bioy Casares, and Ernesto Sabato. Two
years later, a publishing house under the same name was
established. Each contributed greatly to the expansion of
literature, both national and Latin American, as well as
world literature in translation. By 1940, Argentina had
already established itself as a center of literary production
thanks to the Spanish Civil War, which caused an exodus
of some of the most important publishing houses from
Spain to Argentina. After a period of "cultural darkness"
during Juan Perón's first presidency (1946–55), literary production rose sharply during the 1960s reaching its peak in
1974 with unprecedented numbers of editions printed and
sold nationally. This was due to a growing middle-class
readership, a marked increase in university matriculation,
and an explosion of innovative literature by Argentine
writers, in particular, and of Latin American, in general.
Julio Cortázar's *Rayuela* (1963), translated as *Hopscotch*,
epitomized the writing of the Boom era by inviting the

reader to actively participate by playing hopscotch with the text and thus creating a new order.

This kind of democratic participation in the literary and hence cultural text was later squelched by the 1976 military coup that overthrew Isabel Peron, who had become president upon the death of her husband in 1974. During *la Guerra Sucia,* as it was called by the people, a new kind of censorship took place that was part of the military junta's overall Plan for National Reorganization. The *Proceso,* as the military called it, propelled many of Argentina's best writers into exile, including several who are included in this volume. Mempo Giardinelli and Héctor Tizón spent their years in exile in Mexico City, Luisa Valenzuela in New York, and Cristina Siscar in Paris. This volume celebrates their return to the South and remembers those who could not.

> *Sueño el Sur,*
> *Inmensa luna, su cielo al revés.*

I dream the South, Immense moon, its sky upside down.

And like Piazzolla's "Vuelvo al Sur," I too have dreamed the South. The process of compiling this anthology has allowed me that journey, a journey that could not have been made successfully without the help of my traveling companions, my collaborators. In order to ensure that this journey went beyond Buenos Aires and did not get caught up in what Giardinelli calls *obeliscocentrismo,* I sought out contributions that portrayed the vastness of Argentina's geography and the wealth of its literary resources. Like the early explorers, I tried to find the open veins of Argentina in order to tap into the diverseness of its literature by seeking out new voices while ensuring adequate representation of key figures, past and present. This search produced new writers such as Totah as well as a new kind of creative non-fiction epitomized by the work of Juan José Saer and Rodolfo Rabanal. The volume also reconizes the short, short story (*micro-cuento* or *minficción*) as an important genre within Argentine literature as seen in the epigraph, "Time Travel," by Ana María Shua.

I would like to acknowledge the work of my fellow travelers who brought along their new translations on this journey: Jennifer Croft, Alexandra Falek, Andrea Labinger, Suzanne Jill Levine, Darrell B. Lockhart, Mempo Giardinelli, Marcelo Birmajer, and Beth Pollack. I would also like to thank Rhonda Dahl Buchanan, Marina Harss, Andrea Labinger, Suzanne Jill Levine, Gregory Rabassa, and Joanne M. Yates for graciously agreeing to have their translations republished for this "return trip tango." These acknowledgements would be incomplete without a special thank you to the Museo Xul Solar for granting permission to use Solar's *Vuel Villa* (1936) on the cover of this volume and to Dave Peattie for Whereabouts Press so that we can travel the world vicariously whenever we please.

> *Quiero al Sur,*
> *Su buena gente, su dignidad.*
> I love the South, its wonderful people, its dignity.

I have long loved Argentina for and through its literature, for the unique sounds of its River Plate Spanish called *castellano* with its soft "*yeísmo*" and use of the pronoun "*vos*," for its musical traditions, and for the late Mercedes Sosa whose rendition of the above tango "Volver al sur" will make you long to return even if you have never been there before. As Bruce Chatwin proclaimed in his introduction to *Nowhere Is a Place: Travels in Patagonia* (San Francisco: Sierra Club Books, 1992):

> If we are travelers at all, we are literary travelers. A literary reference or connection is likely to excite us as much as a rare animal or plant; and so we touch on some of the instances in which Patagonia has affected the literary imagination.

It can be said, therefore, that literature comes to life through travel, and travel comes alive when seen through the lens of great literature. *Te quiero Sur. ¡Hasta pronto!*

Jill Gibian

(Excerpt from "Vuelvo al sur," written by Astor Piazzolla and Fernando "Pino" Solanas.)

Time Travel
(from *Botany of Chaos*)
Ana Maria Shua

TIME TRAVEL's not only possible, but also inescapable and never ending. Ever since I was born, I've done nothing but sail toward a rotten destiny. What I'd like to do is stop, stay right here, which isn't too bad: throw out the anchor.

Translated by Rhonda Dahl Buchanan

Old Horse
Héctor Tizón

HE HAD BOUGHT HIM in Formosa. The other man now said to him:

"He can hardly see. He's very old. All that tearing has made his eyes cloudy."

He had bought him almost out of boredom. One of those splurges on the spur of the moment. He had money, liked to spend, and so he bought the colt.

The other man was now saying to him: "It's best to

HÉCTOR TIZÓN (1929–) A native of Yala, Jujy, the northernmost province of Argentian, Tizón is a writer, journalist, judge, and former diplomat. His novels and short stories are imbued with the geography and peoples of the northern provinces of Argentina. His first collection of short stories, *A costado de los rieles,* was published in 1960 in Mexico. His extensive literary works have been translated into English, French, German, Polish, and Russian. Among other awards, he has been honored in Argentina by the Fondo Nacional de las Artes, the Sociedad de Letras Argentinas, and the Premio Konex, and in France with the title of Knight of the Order of Arts and Letters.

shoot him. One of these days he'll trip and fall and suffer even more."

The owner didn't answer; he didn't say a word. He turned and looked away. It was an old horse and would have to be killed. It was the law. But he let the days go by. It pained him to see the horse suffer, to see him, old, defeated, nearly blind as he'd suddenly lie on the ground, his legs buckling underneath him, resting his noble face, his mouth drooling, half-open—he was tired. But in his dreams he could hear the horse's youthful neighing—standing boldly on his strong legs or crossing the waters of the San Francisco, with his muzzle all speckled like when he was a young horse, and he would ride him to the markets in Volcán.

He had brought him back from Formosa. Their journey across the Chaco province had been hot and grueling. And there, under the trees, during the days and nights that followed, he had learned to love him, as together they crossed jungles and plains, skirting the marshes, steering clear of the pumas. Later on they traveled several times along that same path and the animal would always listen to him talk, on good days and bad days, following the conversation with an ancestral movement of his ears. When they reached the towns there would always be someone who'd try to buy him. The covetous Mataco Indians would stop and stare as he passed by.

Now he was no longer good for anything; he didn't even eat. He had become a wanderer, roaming alone in the mountains—silent and pensive, a friend to the birds, who would come out out by the dozens to ride on his bony back—returning only as the night would begin to fall.

He had once been good for us kids to ride. In those days he was tame, wise, and cautious. He was the only horse that could remain so steady; stable enough for us to stand on his back, all the way to where the secret hives of the *lechiguanas* were hanging. But he'd also get angry sometimes, like when we were too rowdy; and then, as if he wanted us to get used to it, he'd knock us around a bit. But it was to teach us a lesson. We didn't understand this and when we'd fight back, he wouldn't react; he knew they were children's blows and rather than reacting he'd keep still, staring at us, biting the bit on his bridle, as if he were repressing the pain of injustice.

But now he could no longer see and he'd have to be shot. One day the owner got up the nerve to do it. He left at dawn and went to get him. Together they went to the coast, but he couldn't do it and let him go.

After that he tried two more times. Until the horse understood. The revolver was like a piece of ice paralyzing the owner's hand in his clothing. They arrived at that place along the coast, among the trees. But it wasn't necessary. He stopped by a tree; the old horse jumped up on his legs, gave a youthful, rebellious neigh, and began to gallop around, circling with dizzying speed, frenetically, like an enormous twirling top, until his soul departed and he fell down, dead.

When the owner returned, it was already late. The night had fallen again, and it was dark, yet everyone could see his eyes, red and watery, as if he had been crying.

Translated by Alexandra Falek

For All Eternity
Mempo Giardinelli

HE SHIFTED INTO SECOND and turned onto Route 14 as if angry with the blistering afternoon sun of Corrientes. The Ford F100 seemed to race toward the sky, framed by the Paraná and Uruguay rivers on either side, when Felipe began to tell me the story of his parents' impossible love.

It was a sad story indeed, overly sentimental like all amorous encounters, but with the additional element of tragedy: Felipe's father was only thirty-four when he dropped dead of a heart attack while driving a farm tractor.

"My old lady was ten years younger than he was and

MEMPO GIARDINELLI (1947–) Born in Resistencia, Argentina, in the northern province of Chaco, Giardinelli is not only a prolific writer in his own right, but has done much to foster the dissemination of Argentine literature as editor of numerous anthologies of fiction and the literary magazine *Puro cuento,* which he directed from 1986 to 1992. The selection offered here is a revised version of the story previously published in *El castigo de Dios* (1994).

they had only been married for one. I'm sure they were virgins when they got married, as was the practice back then," Felipe said, shifting into third. "They went to Curitiba, Brazil, on their honeymoon and upon returning they settled down here. They must have shared a few months of wedded bliss, during which time they worked on bringing me into the world. Everything was perfect until the devil reared his ugly head: my old man died exactly two weeks before I was born."

We had been drinking *mate* in the grand old house, prepared for us by la Negra Augusta, Felipe's now aged nursemaid. We sat watching the grief-stricken country folk, caught up in that austere *correntino* mourning that was guarded by figures of saints and tall pillar candles everywhere we turned. Death in Corrientes is so much more than a merely foreseeable event in one's life. Death, around these parts, is a constantly refreshed and definitive tragedy that impacts families during a nine-day period of prayers and psalmodies that disrupt even the surrounding air.

Doña María Luisa had passed away the week before. Everyone at the ranch was subdued, as if the sun no longer shone, as if mourning had inundated their very souls until even light seemed like darkness.

As soon as I got the news I decided to go and spend the weekend with Felipe. Since arriving, two days earlier, we had chewed the fat and recalled our times together at the university, where we studied and shared other rituals: *mate*, barbecues, gin, women, and endless hours of laid-back meaningless conversations.

I soon realized, however, that something was eating at

Felipe. It wasn't just grief; it was rage. He finally opened up to me on the third afternoon, when we had driven into town for supplies and were returning along the dirt road that led back to the ranch house.

"She was an exemplary mother. She raised me to be a man, instilling the values of hard work and study by knocking them into me. It was all well and good, my friend, and yet . . ."

He fell silent and I saw his eyes were overcome with sadness. Either that or it was deep-seated rage, or the idea that was already brewing in his head, or both.

"As a boy I didn't understand. But over the years my old lady's modesty grew more and more incomprehensible. Since I studied in Corrientes, I came to see her every weekend and during vacations, and I watched her become a woman. I saw her reach her sexual peak, but she was always repressed. I saw that she was sought after, but remained ever virtuous. She was painfully virtuous, like all widows back then."

When we sat down to drink a few *mates* that had been waiting for us, he pretended to forget about it by talking about some calves that were stranded in a marsh near Virasoro. I kept quiet and discreetly changed the leafy-green *yerba* in the *mate* so that nothing would distract him from the monologue he was weaving.

"I became a man, my friend, and I realized that beyond my own probable jealousy as a son, that it was natural for my old lady, who turned thirty in full bloom, beautiful—you can't imagine how pretty she was—I mean, it was perfectly natural that she love other men and that lots of other men loved her . . . But man, it was like her womanhood had just died: all that praying all day long, spending all her time in church, and subjecting herself to the sharp tongues of small-town gossips and busybodies, withering away like a daisy wilting in the sun."

He lit up a cigarette and exhaled the smoke as if he were spitting it out.

"And that's how life passed her by. Her virtue was as useless as a dog's lonely baying at the moon. And now she up and dies on me at the still young and bitter age of fifty-four and, man, that ridiculous virtue is the only thing I can't bear."

He rose to his feet and walked toward the gate where a man on horseback had ridden up. He was a typical ranch hand from Corrientes in a black, wide-brimmed hat with a low crown. The man uttered only a few words. Felipe said something in return and the gaucho smoothed his moustache in a respectful gesture and tugged on the reins signaling his chestnut mount to turn back around. He rode off at a slow trot in the same direction he had come, heading toward the paved road, alongside the Uruguay River. Felipe returned with his head down and his brow furrowed.

"Condolences," he said bitterly as he sat down next to me on the bench accepting another *mate*.

I noticed that the afternoon was gradually fading behind a eucalyptus grove.

"Look how nice the sunset's going to be," I told him, changing the subject.

"The only thing people around here know how to do is vote without knowing what they're voting for and deliver condolences," Felipe said, as if he hadn't heard me.

We remained silent for a spell as the sun sank behind the trees and tinged the afternoon with still more sadness. I was amazed by the sight of that enormous red globe being swallowed up by the horizon as if at the point where the earth meets the sky there was an implacable swamp that murdered the day every evening.

Felipe spat a white ball of phlegm that, with rare marksmanship, passed between the wires of the chicken coop at a distance of several yards and said: "As for me, I believe in love, and the day before yesterday I came to the decision to go the cemetery tonight with Augusta and set things right. If you'd like to come . . ."

I nodded confirming that of course I'd come although I had no idea what Felipe had in mind. He looked at me as if I had understood. In his eyes there was a look of surprise mixed with gratitude. At least, that's how it seemed to me.

We ate some delicious pan-fried eel for dinner followed by the unavoidable regional dessert: a thick slice of cheese topped with papaya jam.

We took off, after having coffee and a few shots of gin. It was late, around eleven thirty at night, which is a very advanced hour for what people are accustomed to here. Everyone was asleep, except for us and la Negra Augusta, who had put on a pair of baggy gaucho trousers and showed up at the pickup with a toolbox and trucker's lantern.

We passed through town and kept on going, toward Libres, about five more kilometers. Felipe parked the pickup near the main gate of the cemetery, which was a small field about two hectares in size and enclosed by a simple barbed-wire fence. We walked until Augusta came to a stop in front of a pair of tombs: one constructed of old masonry, the other very recent.

We all three crossed ourselves, respectfully, and Felipe right away opened the box and took out a crescent wrench and some pliers. The headstone of his father's grave gave him more trouble, naturally, because the bolts were rusted in place.

Augusta and I watched him work. The silence, shattered only by the banging on the metal, was overwhelming.

When Felipe had finished the task and lifted both gravestones, he and Augusta set out to remove the lid from both caskets. I remained a mute—and, I must confess, frightened—witness who did nothing. I offered no help nor did they ask for it.

"Mamá is still intact," Felipe murmured, as if he meant only for Augusta to hear him.

As far as I could tell it was true. The cadaver, dressed entirely in white and with her black hair drawn back into an impeccably tight bun, let off a foul, repugnant odor, which was the only thing that felt out of place, curiously enough, on that beautiful night with the full moon and starry sky illuminating the heavens.

The other coffin contained little more than bones. The skeleton was enormous and revealed that Felipe's father had been a tall, strapping bulk of a man. Or this was how I pictured him as I stared aghast in muted silence.

It was then that the most remarkable part of that unforgettable night occurred.

Felipe and Augusta lifted the cadaver of Doña María Luisa, which exhibited the rigidity of a ridiculous-looking mannequin, though at the same time it was quite fragile.

It seemed to me that the body might easily break into pieces during the transfer. The fact that it didn't was due, in all likelihood, to the swiftness with which they flipped it over and placed it, face down, on top of the skeleton in the other grave.

Felipe made some minor adjustments, stood up and stared at his parents, or what remained of them.

Then, he bent over once more to straighten the folds of his mother's dress and spent some time in that position arranging the two cadavers.

I realized that what Felipe was doing was aligning the pelvises of the two bodies.

La Negra Augusta launched into the recitation of a Hail Mary with the murmur of a hoarse songbird.

Felipe closed the two caskets and then replaced both headstones. In the moonlight I could see a look of unmistakable serenity on his face, one of immense relief.

Augusta was still praying as we left the cemetery and climbed into the pickup.

As he turned the key to start the ignition, Felipe looked through the windshield into the night sky as if searching for something in the firmament. I don't know what he was looking for nor if he found it, but he let out a long heavy sigh and as he steered the pickup onto Route 14 he announced to himself, to us and the night, and to no one in particular, that now, at long last, he's got them pelvis to pelvis, damn it, making love for all eternity.

Translated by Darrell B. Lockhart

How Can I Go Back?

Hebe Uhart

I'M NOT A REAL BIG TALKER, and don't think what I'm saying is something I'd tell just anyone, especially not in my village. I'm telling you because you're a stranger; if I told someone from back home, in two minutes I'd be lost. I live on a street right off the main road. My husband and I have a gas station there; it's going well, thank God. He's a good man, and he doesn't let me lack for anything: I've got my fridge, my TV, and a nice little used car—we don't drive it much. The kids went off to live in Venado Tuerto, to go to high school there. My husband and I run the gas station. I also take care of the school: I'm the teacher, the principal, and the custodian—I've got ten students in

HEBE UHART (1936–) was born in Moreno, a province of Buenos Aires. With a quiet starkness, her short stories depict the poverty and alienation of the lower classes and their desire to rise above the harsh circumstances with which they are confronted. Her portraits, often of women, contrast characters from urban and provincial Argentina. This story is from *Camilo asciende y otros relatos* (2004).

all. The place where I live is just four blocks of houses; in winter, by eight o'clock everyone's indoors. And now that I'm far away, looking at it from here, I can't figure out how I managed to live twenty years in that place. It should be no big surprise, because I was born somewhere pretty much like that, off the main road. Lots and lots of cars passed along that road, and I used to stand on a fence gate watching them go by, wishing and hoping (a child's innocence) that some car would stop and take me along. I had no special place in mind: anywhere at all. I'd stand on the fence gate so they'd see me, and I'd say, "Someone's going to notice me." The cars passed like a sigh, and it took me a long time to realize that no one was going to notice me or even look at me, and when I felt all alone and stranded there, it was sort of a disappointment. So I should've grown a thicker skin, but later, when I first got married, I felt that bitterness again. I remember thinking one day at the beginning, What if the gas station caught fire? A big fire, let's say. We'd have no choice but to go live someplace else. But I was already grown up, and a person becomes more sensible; you learn to recognize bad thoughts, put them aside. I never told my husband any of this: he's got a different character, more even-tempered. He's always satisfied, and, really, he has no vices. But lately, after so many years living there, a little of that sadness from my early marriage has returned, and at night, in winter, I look out the window. There's not a soul around, and it makes me feel . . . I don't know. So when the letter came, telling us we'd won the lottery to go to Embalse—the school kids and me—I waited a while before showing it to my husband, partly because I was so confused and didn't know if it was true. Then he got mad at me because I hadn't told him right away. And I pretended I didn't care all that much, because if I let on how much the trip meant to me, everything might've been ruined. Besides, I like people who are settled, calm, reasonable: even on TV you can see what people are like. I watch the actors and artists, and I can tell if they're trustworthy, responsible people, or if they're blowhards, just a lot of hot air. In the letter it said that you should bring along casual clothes, but I figured I ought to take a dress, and since I'd packed all the clothes for the school kids, I chose a dress that was just ordinary. You can see how my face is all leathery from the wind, but not my hands—my hands look like this from washing. When night rolls around and I've finished doing everything, before I sit down to watch TV, I start washing. Over there, evenings are so sad. Sometimes I wish I could make time go faster so night would come right away. Then I say, "I've got to do something useful." And I start washing or tidying up. In the evening those sad thoughts take over, and not even the TV distracts me. Well, when I arrived here in Embalse, I never imagined there could be something like this in the entire world. I would've gladly spent my whole life in Embalse; I never wanted to go back. The first day I arrived, I found myself lost in this big, open space full of people. We didn't talk to anyone, but we figured there must be folks from Buenos Aires, from Entre Ríos, Salta, El Chaco, and so many other places. We went round and round the whole place, trying to find out where to buy pastries and postcards— not like the store back home. Here there are lots of busi- nesses, all crowded together, rows of donkeys and horses with their caretakers; the swings and teeter-totters are full, and all those groups of people exercising.

Then I talked to the teachers from El Chaco. They came over to talk to me and said it was a real pleasure for them to be here because they got their lunches served, and besides they didn't have to go to school. They walked three hours coming and three hours going; along the way they stopped to drink *mate* and use the facilities. "We're easy-going," they told me, "not like those *Porteños*," pointing to the coordinator of the group from the Capital, "always in such a hurry." I had already noticed the coordinator, who from far away looked like a young girl, but from close up I saw she might've been around my age, although it's true she did have hands like a child and long hair, too. She acts like no one's going to notice her and like she doesn't care at all. She goes on the teeter-totter and doesn't eat all the food they serve her in the dining room. She eats from her own bag. I overheard her saying, like it was something bad, "Those people who keep their TV on at home all day long," and I thought, I keep mine on all day long, but it's for company. Although sometimes I don't turn it off because I think: "Now something really nice is going to come on; I don't want to miss it." And the kids from Buenos Aires that she brought with her, they figured out a way to communicate between rooms. The very first day they went out alone to buy pastries, and they arranged with the caretaker to rent horses to ride, and they paid him, all by themselves. I told my students, "Don't wander off too far." But it wasn't really necessary, because at first all they did was stare, like me. And all those contests and games they have! I don't know if you went to the *guitar-*

reada that the teachers from Mendoza held outdoors. I was so happy, but at the same time I felt so sad, thinking, How is it possible I never knew about something like this? I felt sad for the lost years. Well, three nights ago (you probably missed it because I didn't see you there), there was a *guitarreada* in the café, with wine and empanadas. I left the kids with Aníbal, the oldest, and I went to the café with the other teachers. The instructors of the village kids also went. I don't know how they put up with them, poor things. They tiptoed past the kids' bedroom window, and one of the kids recognized them. Right away the kids all started shouting out the bedroom window, "Whores, whores!" And to think they teach those children out of pure idealism. I wore my dress, but then I felt a little out of place: everyone was in jogging suits and sneakers. So many young people! Everybody with a guitar and songs, old ones and new ones. They also played a bolero like that song that goes "Don't fence me in . . ." I started chatting with a gym teacher, younger than me. To this day I don't know how I ended up sleeping with him. Never in twenty years of marriage had I been unfaithful to my husband; I never knew another man. And I want you to understand: I'm not a flirt or a slut. I have the greatest respect for my husband, and luckily he'll never find out what happened. But with that gym teacher I felt something different, as if my head had opened up, as if I'd entered another dimension. There he was in his blue jogging suit—I couldn't even tell you if he was handsome or not. I remember him telling me I was an interesting woman, which I didn't believe, and from what little I know of life, I understood from the start that it was just an adventure, nothing more.

Please don't get me wrong: I didn't fall in love—it's not decent to fall in love at my age—and besides, looking at it objectively, you might even say my gym teacher was a little sleazy. I'd never marry a man like that. Later he came around looking for me, but I didn't want anything to do with him: I had plenty to think about as it was. Do you know what I'm thinking about? About how to get back to my village. Here I am: I talk to the teachers from Salta who tell me about their poor lives up there, even poorer than mine; I listen to the loudspeaker and think that if there's a whole world in this place, how much more must there be outside, everywhere, and now that we're about to return, all I do is wonder, how can I go back to my village?

Translated by Andrea G. Labinger

About the Shape of the World
Adolfo Bioy Casares

ONE MONDAY NIGHT in the early fall of '51, a young fellow named Correa, whom many called "The Geographer," was waiting on El Tigre dock for the ferry that would take him to the island of his friend Mercader, where he was planning to withdraw from the world and prepare for his first-year law school exams. The island in question was really a bushy swamp with a little wooden house on piles: an inaccessible place in the enormous delta's labyrinth of riverlets and weeping willows. Mercader had advised him: "Lost out there with only the mosquitoes for company,

---

ADOLFO BIOY CASARES (1914–1999) A frequent collaborator with his friend Jorge Luis Borges, Bioy Casares published many stories with him under the pseudonym of H. Bustos Domecq. He is perhaps best known for his novel *The Invention of Morel* (1940), which blends realism, fantasy, and science fiction. Similarly, the story presented here, translated by Suzanne Jill Levine, takes us on a journey between Argentina and Uruguay where borders and beings take on an ethereal quality.

what else can you do but sink your teeth into your studies? When the time comes, you'll pass with flying colors." Even Dr. Guzmán, an old friend of the family, whom they had charged with keeping a benevolent eye on Correa's activities in Buenos Aires, approved of that brief exile, which he considered most timely and even necessary. Nevertheless, during his three days spent as an islander, Correa did not manage to read the number of pages he had planned. He spent Saturday nursing a roast and sipping *mate,* and on Sunday he went to the soccer game between the Rovers and the Hurricanes, because he frankly didn't feel like opening a book. He had begun his first two nights with the firm intention of working, but sleep soon got the better of him. He remembered those nights as if there had been many, and he resented his futile efforts and belated regrets. On Monday, he had to return to Buenos Aires to have lunch with Dr. Guzmán and go with a group of friends from his native province to the evening show at the Maipo Theater, as he had promised. Now back at El Tigre dock, he waited for the ferry, which was unusually late, and thought that the delay wasn't his fault but that from now on he should make use of every minute, because the date of his first exam was drawing near.

He went anxiously from one worry to the next. What should I do, he wondered, if the boatman doesn't know which island is Mercader's? (The one who had taken him before had known.) I'm not sure I'll recognize it.

The other people on the dock started chatting. Away from the group, leaning on the rail, Correa looked at the groves of trees on the other bank, blurry in the night. It's true that in broad daylight they would have been just as confusing to him, since he was new to the place; it didn't look like anything he had seen ever before, but like a landscape often imagined and dreamed of: the Malay archipelago, as revealed to him in the classrooms of his native province by more than one Salgari picture book, covered in brown paper so that the priests would think it was a textbook.

When it began to rain, he had to take shelter under the awning, near the talkers. He very soon discovered that they weren't all in one group, as he had presumed, but rather there were three, or at least three. A girl, hanging on the arms of a man, was complaining: "Then you don't know how I feel." The man's answer was lost behind a trembling voice that was saying: "The project, which now seems so simple, met with great resistance, because of the erroneous notion people had about continents." After a pause, the same voice (perhaps with a Chilean accent) continued in a tone suggesting good news: "Fortunately Carlos gave Magellan his full support." Correa wanted to follow the couple's exchange, but a third conversation, on the subject of smugglers, dominated the others and brought to mind a book about smugglers or pirates that he had never read because it bored him from the start, illustrated with pictures of characters from long ago, dressed in baggy pants, riding coats, and shirts that were too large.

He said to himself that he would begin studying as soon as he reached the island. He thought that he would be very tired, that he wouldn't be able to concentrate, that he would fall asleep on the books. The wisest thing would be to set the alarm for three o'clock and have a little nap—

nice and comfortable, on the cot of course—and then, refreshed, undertake his reading assignments. With a sinking feeling he imagined the ringing bell, the ungodly hour. "No need to get discouraged," he thought. "Since there's nothing else to do on the island except study, when exam time comes around, I'll pass with flying colors."

Someone asked him: "What's your opinion?"

"About what?"

"Smuggling."

One would think (but we know now what happened) that the wisest thing would have been to get out of it with a neutral answer that wouldn't compromise him. He was carried away by the discussion, and before he could think, he was saying: "As far as I'm concerned, smuggling is not a felony."

"Uh-huh," the other man commented. "Then what, may I ask, is it?"

"As far as I'm concerned," Correa insisted, "it's a simple violation."

"What you say interests me," said a tall gentleman with a white moustache and glasses.

"Let me tell you," someone shouted, "blood is spilled over that violation."

"Soccer has its martyrs too," complained an enormous man who seemed to be wearing a tight-fitting beret, but it was only curly hair.

"And it's not a crime, as far as I know," the man with the white moustache and glasses said. "In soccer, you must separate the pros from the amateurs. In smuggling, does the gentleman consider himself professional, amateur, or what? The point interests me."

"I'll go even further," Correa insisted. "As far as I'm concerned, smuggling is the inevitable violation of an arbitrary order. Arbitrary, like everything the state does."

"By such personal opinions," someone remarked, "the gentleman makes himself out to be a downright anarchist."

Such personal opinions were actually Dr. Guzmán's. Correa had not only faithfully repeated Guzmán's words but had even imitated his voice.

From the other corner of the group, a tidy little fat man—a professional man, probably a dentist, Correa thought—smiled at him as if congratulating him. As to the others, they no longer spoke to him; they spoke about him, probably disapprovingly.

After a while the ferry arrived. Correa was not sure of its name. *Victory Something-or-other,* he thought. It was obviously some kind of river bus that had been going up and down the delta for a long time.

As they all pushed to board the ferry, he accidentally bumped into the little fat man, who smiled and asked: "Have you ever seen a smuggler?"

"As far as I know, never."

The man raised his hands to his lapels, stuck out his chest, and stated: "You've got one right in front of you."

"You don't say."

"But I do say. You can call me Dr. Marcelo."

"Dentist?"

"You guessed it: *odontologist.*"

"And a smuggler in your spare time."

"I'm sure—in reference to the reasons you explained so admirably—that in this capacity I'm not harming a soul.

No one except businessmen and the taxman, and I'm not going to lose any sleep over them, believe you me. I earn a few pesos, almost as much as at the office, but in a way that for the moment is more fun because it borders on adventure, something new for a man like me. Or like you, I'd be willing to bet."

"Do you know me?"

"I'm judging by appearances. You seem like a nice fellow, a bit shy, but with the right stuff. You people from inland are better, when not worse . . . Although with today's youth, *chi lo sa*, who knows?"

"You don't trust young people? Don't think that just because someone's young he gets involved with the nonsense and stupidity all around him."

"I don't think that way. That's why I spoke to you as I did."

"Maybe you're sorry now. Maybe you think I'll tell the cops on you."

"Not in the slightest. It's just that I spoke to you as if I knew you, and I really don't."

To put the dentist at ease, Correa told him who he was: He was studying law; he was preparing for his second year; he was going to stay at his friend's island for a couple of weeks; he was new to this area.

"All I know is that I have to get off after an amusement park called Encarnación. I'm afraid of not recognizing the place and passing it by. And if I do get to where I'm going, a tough dilemma awaits me: Should I study or sleep?"

"Marvelous," the dentist exclaimed happily. "You have spontaneously given me, take my word for it, the best proof of your sincerity."

"Why wouldn't I, if I feel like sleeping? Look: I want to study, but I'm so tired I'm falling off my feet."

"Do you want to study? Are you sure?"

"Of course I'm sure."

"Listen, I'm not asking if you want to study in general. I'm asking if you want to study tonight."

Correa considered the dentist an intelligent man, and said: "The truth is, tonight I really don't feel like it."

"Then sleep. The best thing is to sleep. Unless . . ."

"Unless what?"

"Nothing, nothing, an idea I haven't quite chewed over yet."

As if talking to himself, Correa murmured: "It's not nice to begin a sentence . . ."

"Careful what you say. Remember, you're talking to a professional. A university graduate."

"I didn't mean to offend you."

"Sometimes I wonder if the best method to educate people isn't to give them a good kick in the ass."

"Don't take it so hard."

"That's my business. You irritated me, just when I was going to make you an offer, with the best intentions."

At Encarnación almost all the people who before had been arguing about smuggling got off noisily.

After thinking awhile, Correa asked: "What offer were you going to make?"

"A third alternative for that rough dilemma."

"Forgive me, sir, I'm not following you. What dilemma?"

"Sleep or study. And you, young man, even in your dreams you have to call me Doctor."

Correa thought, or simply felt, that an offer that would give him a way out of the decision between sleep and study was tempting. He was about to say yes, when he remembered the doctor's activities.

"Before accepting your offer, I'm going to ask you to explain something. And please, be frank"

"Are you suggesting that I'm not frank?"

"Not at all."

"Go ahead, ask."

"Don't think I'm afraid, but what if something happens to me and I can't study, or I don't make it to the exam? It would be a real mess. Will I be in danger? Will I be running risks?"

"One is always in danger of the unexpected, so that for the coward there is only one piece of advice: Stay in your little hole. Don't leave your house. But in this case you are traveling like a crowned head, incognito, so you're not running the slightest risk."

Before Correa agreed, the doctor had already accepted him as his companion and started to give him all sorts of explanations, which to Correa were irrelevant. The doctor said that he lived with his wife on an island; that a fast-talking auctioneer had proposed a business transaction, another island, which wasn't far from his; that he let him go on, although he had no intention of buying it, because nothing went against him more than letting money out of his hands, even for a solid investment. The day the missus found out about the offer, he didn't have a moment's peace.

"The missus is full of spirit," he explained. "You won't believe it. Her engine's running all the time, and from the first she was fanatically in favor of buying the island. She began to say to me: 'One must always expand. The island is a big step.' In my own way, I'm stubborn too, so I let her talk, but I didn't give in an inch, not until the last Sunday of the past month, when some friends of my wife stopped by to visit, and I said to myself: 'Why not go out to the island and have a look?' I took off in my private boat. When I arrived, the caretaker, who was listening to a soccer game, told me to please take a look by myself, though there wasn't much to see."

At that point in his story, the doctor paused, and then added with an air of mystery: "The caretaker was wrong."

If there was a mystery, Correa didn't believe it. Nevertheless, he suspected that the doctor was talking to him to keep him busy, to keep him from looking at the shore and remembering or recognizing landmarks on the way. The truth is, for all he stared at those unknown places that kept going by, they all looked identical and were hopelessly mixed together like the parts of a dream.

"Why was the caretaker wrong?"

"You'll see. My grandfather, who built up a respectable fortune in Poland, but who then had to emigrate, used to say: 'Seek and ye shall find. Even when there is nothing, if you look hard enough you'll find what you want.' He'd also say: 'The best places for a searcher are attics and the far corners of gardens.' This island might not be a garden, but . . ."

"But what?"

"Now we're getting off," the doctor said. Immediately he shouted: "Boatman, stop here, please."

The dock, its wood rotting, was small and doubtlessly unsteady. Correa looked at it apprehensively.

"I'm doing the wrong thing," he moaned. "I, sir, should be studying."

"Go on with that 'sir' business. You know better than I that you weren't going to study tonight. Stop the nonsense and kindly follow me. Be careful to step where I step. See the little house there among the willows? That's where the caretaker lives. Don't be afraid, there's no dog."

"You swear?"

"I swear. That man's only friend is the radio. Here on the island, walk only where I walk. We have to stay on solid ground, so as not to leave tracks. I'll bet that if I didn't say anything you'd head for the mud, like the pigs."

With his hands up high, the doctor pushed aside the branches to clear the way. It seemed to Correa that they were descending a slope into twilight, a twilight that gradually became pitch-dark, as if they were in a tunnel underground. He realized that he was, precisely, in a tunnel: a long, narrow tunnel with a floor of leaves, and walls and a roof of leaves and branches, except at the deepest part, which was really underground and where there was absolute darkness. The place seemed unpleasant, especially because it was strange and unexpected. He wondered why he had allowed himself to be taken away from his duty. Who was his companion? A smuggler, a delinquent whom nobody in his right mind would trust. The worst was that Correa depended on this man, and he believed that if he abandoned him he would not be able to find the way out. An irrational idea, which seemed obvious, came to mind: The tunnel was infinite at both ends. Correa was beginning to feel extremely anxious, when he suddenly found himself outside. The journey had lasted no more than three or four minutes. Above ground it would have been a matter of seconds. They were in a totally different place from what they had left at the other end of the tunnel. Correa described it as a "garden city," an expression he had heard more than once but whose meaning escaped him. They walked along a winding road, lined with gardens and white houses with red roofs.

The doctor reproached him: "Did you come with only Argentine money? I figured as much. They'll change your money anywhere, but don't let them cheat you. I know where you can get a good exchange rate and where they sell merchandise that you can sell for a profit in Buenos Aires. Such knowledge, you understand, has its price, so don't think I'm going to tell you for nothing. Someday, who knows, we may be partners. For the time being, every man for himself. See that sign?"

"The number fourteen bus stop?"

"That's the one. We'll meet there Wednesday morning at five o'clock sharp."

Correa protested. This wasn't what they had agreed on. He had resigned himself to missing one night and now he was going to miss two nights and a day.

The doctor took a step back, as if he wanted to take a good look at him. "Just what do you think you're suggesting? That we return in broad daylight to publish our secret to the whole world? Do you know that if I'm not careful you might cost me dearly? Now tell me, what will you do in a foreign country without my protection? Will you start crying? Will you ask the consul to send you back to your country in a trunk?"

Correa realized he was at the doctor's mercy and that he'd be better off not to provoke him.

"See you Wednesday," he said.

"See you Wednesday," the doctor said, looking at his watch. "At five sharp, so we'll have enough time, because it gets light at six and I don't like to have to rush. I go this way, and you go that way. Don't you dare try to follow me, because I'll brain you."

Correa walked awhile and started thinking that if the doctor missed their appointment, he would find himself in a tight spot. He didn't have much money on him, and he certainly couldn't trust himself to find the mouth of the tunnel. The wisest thing would be to find it before his memory got confused. He tried to retrace his steps, but very soon the winding streets completely disoriented him. There was one detail he had neglected to clarify so as not to sound stupid: Where were they? He was getting dizzy and felt that his state of fatigue it would be better to stop walking in circles on streets built by people who ignored the rudiments of the chessboard design. He also realized that what he needed most was to sleep a little. Then he would face the situation. "I'll lie down and sleep anywhere," he said out loud, and added, "Anywhere there isn't a dog." Immediately his troubles began: there was at least one dog per garden, if not two, in this place. Perhaps to appease his guilty conscience, he thought that if instead of committing the stupid mistake of listening to the doctor he had returned to Mercader's island, as any person with an ounce of sense would have done, he would not have been able to study in such a tired state. If he did not find a garden without a dog soon, he would sleep in the street. Fearfully, he entered the gates of a villa and walked under a laurel bower, which looked ghostly in the light of dawn. Since no dog was barking, he lay down to sleep.

When he awoke, the sun was in his eyes. He was startled to notice that someone was looking at him from close up. It was a young woman; she wasn't unattractive, and her face seemed flushed. As he was nervous, he confusedly thought he should calm her down.

"Excuse me for coming in," he said. "I was so tired that I went to sleep. Don't be afraid, I'm not a thief."

"I don't care what you are," the woman answered. "Would you like something? You must be hungry at this hour, but you'll have to settle for breakfast. Today, I didn't make a thing."

They walked through the grass and bushes, until they came to a white house with a red tile roof, surrounded by a veranda with red paving stones. Inside, it was shaded and cool.

"My name's Correa," he said.

The woman answered that her name was Cecilia, and she added a surname, which sounded perhaps like Viñas, but in another language. Apparently, they were alone in the house.

"Sit down," the woman said. "I'll go make breakfast."

Correa thought about that strange tunnel: it was definitely very short, but the way things looked it had taken him very far, and he wondered where he was. He rose and wert down a hallway to the kitchen. Cecilia, her back to him, was busy boiling water and toasting bread; she did not turn around immediately. She quickly ran her hand across her face.

"I'm going to ask you something," Correa announced, but he was silent and then said: "What's the matter?"

"My husband left me," Cecilia explained, crying. "See, nothing special."

He again put off his question, to comfort the woman, but he found it difficult. It got even worse as he found out more and more about her situation. Cecilia loved her husband, who had left her for a younger and prettier woman.

"Now I know he had always deceived me, so that not even a good memory of my great love is left."

Cecilia did not stop crying, and Correa said to himself that perhaps it was inappropriate to point out to her that the water was boiling. When they smelled the burnt toast, she smiled despite the tears. Correa liked her smile, partly because it interrupted the tears. These, unfortunately, soon began falling again, and Correa caressed her because he couldn't find arguments that would comfort her, and he discovered that the tears served to stimulate the caresses, which Cecilia repaid in kind, until some unforeseeable word must have evoked memories that threatened to bring on a relapse.

When he was preparing for the worst, Cecilia remarked: "Now I'm hungry too. I'm going to cook something."

A lot of tears, but she's good-natured, Correa thought. They ate, took a nap together, and it seemed there was time for everything. The first moment he remembered Dr. Marcelo, he thought: Just as long as he doesn't miss our appointment . . . Then he was afraid the time to leave would come too soon, and he found his observation of the fact that Cecilia accepted his caresses not only cynical but also vulgar and stupid. It's precisely because she feels pain that she needs to be comforted, he thought; caresses, as crying children prove, are the universal consolation. He forgot the doctor, he forgot his exams. He discovered that he liked Cecilia an awful lot.

That long day, which gave him so many things, also gave him the opportunity to ask: "Where are we?"

Cecilia answered: "What do you mean?"

"What part of the world are we in?"

"In Uruguay, of course. In Punta del Este."

Correa needed a moment to understand what he'd been told. Then he asked: "How far is Punta del Este from Buenos Aires?"

"It's like Mar del Plata. The plane takes about the same time."

"How many miles is that?"

"About three hundred fifty."

Correa told her she knew a lot, but there was something he knew that she might not know. "I'll bet you don't know there's a tunnel where you can walk from here, very easily, with no hurry whatsoever, in five minutes."

"From where?"

"From El Tigre, of course. The delta itself. Do you think I'm lying? Last night, with a doctor named Marcelo, I left El Tigre, took a boat a little ways, and reached an island covered with poplar trees and bushes, the same as any other. There, hidden away, was the mouth of a tunnel. We went inside, and even though underground it seemed an eternity, it didn't take us five minutes to come out again in a garden city, full of parks."

"Punta del Este."

"You said it. I must add that the tunnel is a secret to the whole world, except the doctor, you, and me. Please don't tell anybody else."

Fascinated with his own explanations, he didn't notice that Cecilia was sad again.

"I'm not going to tell anybody," she assured him. In a different tone she remarked: "No matter how good a companion he is, you're always alone with a liar."

Correa explained in earnest: "I don't know how anyone could have ever felt like lying to you."

Suddenly, out of the blue, he was overwhelmed by the intolerable fear that Cecilia thought the tunnel was a lie. Just in case, he began to give a more detailed account of the journey that night, from his meeting with Dr. Marcelo until they went their separate ways at the number 14 bus stop. He indicated emphatically: "Right at that stop, tomorrow morning at five o'clock sharp, the doctor will be waiting for me, to take me back."

"Through the tunnel?" Cecilia said, on the edge of tears.

"I have to go study. There're only a few days left before exams. I'm in law school."

"Why that whole story? I'll get used to men abandoning me."

"It's not a story. On the contrary: I have spontaneously given you the best proof of my sincerity. If Dr. Marcelo finds out, he'll kill me."

"Come on—it's as if I told you I came from Europe in a tunnel in five minutes."

"That's different. Listen: Between us and Europe there are many miles and lots of water. If you still don't believe me, I'm going to ask Dr. Marcelo to explain everything, so that next week, when I come back, I'll be able to explain the whole thing to you."

As if talking to herself, Cecilia said: "When you come back."

To gain time, until finding a decisive answer, he held her in his arms. The best part of that day was very happy and lasted a long time—more than the day itself, it seemed to him. Although an alarm clock hurried along on the night table, they could believe that time would never run out. But suddenly the house grew dark, and Correa went to the window and, without knowing why, felt sad when he saw twilight.

The night had further happiness in store for them. They ate something (he remembered it as a feast), they went back to bed, and again it seemed as if time were stretching. They got hungry, and when Cecilia went to the kitchen, Correa set the alarm clock for four-thirty. They ate fruit, talked, fell into each other's arms, and must have fallen asleep, because the alarm clock startled them.

"What's that?" she asked. "Why?"

"I set the alarm. He's waiting for me, remember?"

Cecilia hesitated before answering: "That's right. At five o'clock sharp."

Correa got dressed. He hugged her and pushed her away a little so he could took into her eyes. He promised: "I'm coming back next week."

Although he was sure he was coming back, he was annoyed by Cecilia's doubts; apparently, she didn't believe in the tunnel or the promises. "I would have liked you to accompany me to the 14 so you could see with your own eyes that Dr. Marcelo is no invention of mine. Since you're not coming, show me the way, please."

Cecilia was more interested in hugging him than in giving him directions.

Finally, he left. More than once, he thought he was lost, but he reached the appointed spot. Nobody was there. What a mess if the doctor has left already, he thought. What a mess if I don't make it to my exams.

He would feel a little ashamed to have to go back to Cecilia's and tell her that he had very little money and, until he got work, wouldn't be able to pay his part of the expenses. Maybe such a speech would be a silly formality, because they both loved each other, but a formality is an annoyance to a person who has the reputation for being a liar. He admitted, however, that the situation wasn't so serious; Cecilia would be happy, and if they lived together their misunderstandings would soon disappear. Absorbed in his fantasies and without paying much attention, he saw a man coming toward him. The fellow had been approaching for a while, arduously dragging two big packages.

"Why the hell don't you help me?" the man shouted.

Surprised, Correa excused himself: "I didn't see you."

The doctor wiped his forehead with a handkerchief and sighed. Then he said: "You didn't buy anthing? I had the feeling you wouldn't. You didn't bring any money, which I thought was wrong, and you didn't ask me for a loan, which I thought was correct, perfectly correct. On our next excursion you'll start making profits. Now help me carry this."

As well as he could, Correa carried both bags, which were quite heavy. So as not to trip, he kept his eyes fixed on the ground, or more precisely, on where he stepped.

"I was afraid you wouldn't come," he said.

He almost couldn't talk; he was panting. The doctor replied: "I was afraid *you* wouldn't come. Do you know what those bags weigh? Now I feel like I have wings, believe you me. It's a pleasure to walk. Come on, let's go."

In the middle of the tunnel, Correa had to stop to rest, and he remarked: "What I don't understand is how, through here, through this simple tunnel, Punta del Este and El Tigre are so close together."

"Not El Tigre," the doctor corrected him, "but the island that I'm going to buy with my savings."

"It's the same thing, for all practical purposes. If a plane takes an hour to get from Punta del Este to Buenos Aires . . ."

"I won't beat around the bush: Planes just don't convince me. Through the tunnel I get there right away, without spending a red cent, you realize."

"That's what I don't understand. If we start off with the premise that the earth is round . . ."

"Who cares about premises. You say it's round because they told you that, but you don't really know if it's round, square, or like your own face. I'm warning you: If geographical details are all you can think of, don't count on me. At my age I don't have the patience for such stupidity. I wonder if taking you on as a partner wasn't a big mistake. A man like you, who's so out of touch with reality, might kick around my tunnel with women and strangers."

"How could you think I would kick those things around? And what's more, with strangers."

"With nobody," the doctor stressed, looking at him piercingly.

"With nobody."

"If that's the case, carry the bags and stop wasting time."

They came out on the island: Correa saw the sky and felt mud under his feet. They walked past willows, then a row of poplars. Correa could barely keep moving.

"Are you taking me to the thickest part on purpose?" he asked.

"Don't you understand that we're looking for a place to hide the packages? Or would you like us to take them on the ferry, in full view of everybody?"

They finally reached a field of reeds that the doctor took to be sufficient.

"Here, not even God will find them," Correa asserted.

"I didn't ask your opinion."

Correa let that insolence pass and asked: "How long are you going to leave them here?"

"I'm coming for them tonight, in my private boat. But you're very curious. Are you itching to steal what's not yours?"

Correa asked angrily: "Who do you take me for?"

The doctor lost his poise and excused himself: "It was a joke. A mere joke. I hope the ferry comes soon. I must say that I don't really feel very comfortable in these swamps. Besides, I wouldn't like anybody to see us here. It's going to get light any minute now, and we'll be exposed to the first nosybody. I must tell you that I think the missus is right: I should buy the island. As soon as possible, because when you least expect it, some bum who has nothing to do is going to wonder. What's that guy up to, going twice a week to an island that doesn't belong to him? I'm not in favor of throwing money away, mind you, but this time I'll pay with my eyes shut."

"You're right," Correa remarked. "It would be terrible if something unpleasant happened."

When the ferry appeared, they called out. The doctor paid for the tickets; they hadn't settled in their seats when he was already demanding: "I'm waiting for you to pay your debt. A moment's distraction, and a person gets eaten alive."

Correa gave him a ten-peso bill. That was a lot of money in those days. He said: "Take what I owe you."

"You want to take all my change?"

"I gave you what I have."

The doctor looked annoyed. Then he patted his pocket and with sudden contentment stated: "It's safer here. You'll get your change the next time."

"When do we go back?"

He didn't get an answer, and he didn't dare repeat the question. For a while they said nothing.

"If you're stopping at Mercader's house," the doctor finally said, "you'd better get on deck, because these boatmen don't lose any time."

Correa obeyed, and asked: "Then we're not going back?"

The doctor pushed him rudely. "You're impossible," he

complained. "Whisper, if you don't want half the world to know. We'll meet Thursday, same time, same place. Okay?"

Correa could barely contain his joy. He said to himself that things were looking up. Cecilia expected him the following week, but he would arrive Friday at dawn and give her a surprise that he considered very special. He was about to jump to the ground when he wondered whether he had overlooked anything. He was frightened by the possibility of missing the doctor. He murmured: "At eleven-thirty?"

"Fine."

"At El Tigre?"

"If you know and I know," the doctor interrupted him, trembling with rage, "why do we have to let everybody else know? Get off, do me the favor, get off."

From the shore Correa watched the ferry disappear. Then he walked to the house, ran up the stairs with great strides, opened the door, and stood there, to arm himself with courage, because he knew that when he entered that room the wait would begin. The long and impatient wait for his second trip to Uruguay. He commented aloud: "I don't know what's wrong with me. I'm nervous." He obviously didn't feel like studying. So as not to waste time—every minute until exam day was precious—the best thing was to sleep a while. He would give himself over fully to his studies when he had calmed down and refreshed himself.

As soon as he dropped onto the cot, he realized that he also didn't feel like sleeping. He said to himself that it would be a long time before Thursday arrived, and centu-

ries before Friday, when he would see Cecilia: before then
things could happen that were better not to think about.
He thought about his appointment at El Tigre; about the
possibility that the doctor, because of any kind of trouble,
might not appear. With the little information he had, it
would not be easy to get in touch with him. He didn't
even know his last name. If the doctor didn't appear on
Thursday, Correa would have no choice but to stand there
waiting on the dock until the doctor felt like putting in an
appearance. What if the doctor didn't return to El Tigre,
if from now on he went straight from his house to the
island of the tunnel entrance? Correa thought that the
wisest thing was to go that very evening to wait for the
doctor beside the packages. This way, at least, he would
be sure to see him, since the man would come get them
at nightfall. He wondered if he could recognize the island
on that unknown shore, where a house, a dock, whatever,
got lost in the monotonous succession of trees. It was true
that the sooner he returned, the better were his chances
of identifying it.

He found some money he had been keeping between
the pages of Gide's *Political Economy*. By not returning
his change, the doctor had deprived him not only of a
few pesos, which are always useful, but also the possibility of knowing the price of the trip to the island, which
would have served as a point of reference to find it. Now
he didn't know what to say when asking for his ticket.
He couldn't request a so-and-so-peso ticket or a ticket to
such-and-such a place. He knew few places on the delta
by name.

He brooded over the projected trip. He had to choose

the moment carefully: if he got there when it was still light, someone might see him on the island, and if he got there at nightfall, he might not recognize it. As the hours passed he imagined more vividly the anxieties he would have to face. Who knows how long he'd have to wait crouching beside the packages, among clouds of mosquitoes, in that weed-ridden swamp. What for? He wouldn't even free himself from the fear of not meeting up with the doctor. On the contrary: he saw reasons why his fear would increase after their encounter. Until now, he hadn't given the doctor any reason to complain, but if the doctor suddenly found him on the island, he could never in a thousand years convince him that he wasn't there to rob him or take advantage of his knowledge of the tunnel to work on his own.

On the other hand, if he didn't bother him by appearing unexpectedly, why would the doctor miss their appointment? To keep those few pesos? That didn't seem rational.

The only intelligent decision was to stick to what they'd agreed on. He would stay put, then, until Thursday, as calm as possible, as he should.

He had hardly made that decision when he became terribly restless. He was giving up immediate action, he said to himself, because he was insecure, lazy, and cowardly. He spent Wednesday brooding and making contradictory decisions. Because he couldn't study, he tried to sleep; because he couldn't sleep, he tried to study. On Thursday, he fell asleep at daybreak. When he awoke, it was almost time to meet the doctor. He washed his face and shaved with cold water, put on a clean shirt, dressed quickly, and ran to wait for the ferry that would take him to El Tigre.

Everything went well. At eleven-thirty sharp, as they had agreed, he was waiting on the dock. After a while he said to himself that he should have arrived at eleven, or eleven-fifteen at the latest. Of course if the doctor wanted to avoid him, getting there early wouldn't have done him any good, and if he didn't want to avoid him, he wouldn't leave before it was time. Unless my watch is slow, Correa thought, and he compared it with that of a man who was waiting for the ferry. It wasn't slow.

The ferry arrived. Correa asked if it was the last. There would be another one.

If the doctor didn't come, he would take the last boat and keep his eyes peeled, paying close attention to the coastlines, in order to identify the island. On the island, he would find the mouth of the tunnel easily. With the doctor, things would have been simpler, but he could manage alone to get to where Cecilia was waiting for him.

The doctor didn't come. Correa became superstitious: he thought the doctor wouldn't come until three boats had passed by. The ferry came. He was determined to get on, but how intensely he wanted the doctor to arrive! He was about to jump on board, when he saw a man crossing the street, in the direction of the dock. The man waved his hand, and perhaps shouted something. Only when the man entered the dock and walked in the circle of light from the streetlamp did Correa see that it wasn't the doctor; it didn't even look like the doctor, although both men were short and rather fat.

Incredibly, the stranger spoke to Correa. "You're waiting for someone, right?" he asked.

"That's right."

"A doctor?"

"Dr. Marcelo."

"He couldn't come. Follow me."

After some hesitation. Correa followed him. They went along the river and turned left. Correa could read a street sign: "Tedin Street." There were still people in the doorways.

"Do we have far to go?" he asked.

"Don't tell me you're tired already," the man answered; he seemed less tidy than the doctor, and stronger. "We cross the bridge over the Reconquista, and from there it's not far."

They went along the wall of the State Gas Club. Against the wall, farther on, stood a big man.

Correa stopped a moment and said: "That's not the doctor."

"Not by a long shot. Don't tell me you're suspicious?"

"I'm not suspicious, but . . ."

"There're no ifs or buts here. If you're suspicious, you must have your reasons. Are you following me, or do I have to push you?"

Before following him, Correa quickly looked around.

"It's useless to look: there's nobody around."

"I don't understand."

"You understand. And what's more, let me tell you: Your suspiciousness makes me and this here gentleman, who's a friend, think twice."

The big man looked at him without expression. His head, which was noticeably round, was covered thickly with short black hair. Correa thought he had seen him somewhere before.

"Are you going to attack me?"

Who do you take us for? You think we'd dirty ourselves for the two or three pieces of garbage you've got on you? Don't make me laugh. We're such nice guys that we've gone to the trouble of coming here to give you a piece of advice. Listen: Forget that partner of yours. Forget him. For your own good, get it? That man means trouble for you. Is that clear?"

To gain time and think, because his mind was confused, Correa asked: "The doctor?"

"Yes, the doctor, or whatever the heck you call him. Don't play the fool, because my friend here gets nervous and something could happen to you too. You know who we're talking about: that short, fat guy."

The big man, who had an unexpectedly gentle voice, said: "Listen, you: Do us the favor of forgetting everything you know, and forget about us too, and keep us far away from the places where you've been seen with that doctor. Okay?"

"Sure, why not, okay," said Correa.

When he realized that the danger was less pressing, he remembered Cecilia, and said to himself that he wasn't going to abandon her out of mere cowardice. He shouldn't be afraid of talking, because his was a rather common situation, which anyone could understand. He asked: "Can I be frank with you?"

"Sure, sure," the larger man answered. "As long as it doesn't take you too long."

"What I'm going to tell you is very simple. I'm not looking for the doctor because of any money interests. Do you know why I'm looking for him? So he'll take me to Uruguay, to see a person I left there."

Pointing to him, the big man remarked: "The gentleman is the generous type."

"And lucky too. He has somebody waiting for him in Uruguay."

"And he suffers when he's not with her. The gentleman thinks you and I are dumb."

"Like the doctor thought, may he rest in peace."

"The doctor thought he was a wise guy. He wanted to entertain us with lies."

"Stories, like the person the gentleman has in Uruguay."

Correa complained angrily, first about the things they were saying, then at the fact they were touching him, but he quieted down and barely managed to cover his head with his hands when the beating began.

At some time—much later, as he found out—he was awakened by a man who asked, in an insistent and friendly manner: "What's the matter? Are you ill?"

Helped by the stranger, a tall man with a white moustache and glasses, Correa stood up with great effort. His whole body ached.

He remarked sadly: "I think I've been beaten up."

"Are you going to report it? I'll accompany you, if you wish, to the police station. The police captain is a friend of mine."

"I don't think I feel like going to the police station. With the beating I think I've had enough for one night."

"You're perfectly within your rights. Come home with me for a moment, so I can clean those bruises for you."

Walking painfully, Correa let the man lead him. His house seemed very presentable, with wrought-iron gates and chandeliers, and big colonial chairs.

"Forgive me for being a bother," Correa said.

"Here I'll have enough light to attend to you. Are you comfortable? That's the main thing."

The man made Correa sit down next to a wrought-iron standing lamp, in the corner of a drawing room. Correa thought with gratitude and respect: I'm in the dining room, which is reserved for special occasions. In the middle was a long table of varnished black wood.

The man disinfected his wounds with peroxide and blew on his face carefully.

"It burns," Correa said.

"It's nothing," the man assured him.

"Because it's not burning you."

"I won't dispute that. You should realize, however, that you got away with it easy, if you take into consideration what happened to the other guy. Follow me? And don't think they are bad boys."

"Do you know them?" Correa asked, surprised.

The man smiled amiably.

"Here, everybody knows everybody else," he explained. "The boys, as I was saying, aren't bad: a bit nervous, the result of youth. You shouldn't have lied to them."

"I didn't lie."

"Going to Uruguay, to see a woman—it's an old story."

"But it's not a lie."

"My good man, let me make this perfectly clear: If you find yourself in an argument with serious people, you'd do better not to come out with nonsense. It's natural, it's only human, that our friends would get excited. Besides, why did you need the doctor at your side to visit a woman?"

"The doctor knows an island where there's a tunnel."

At this point, everything speeded up.

"You mean a cave, a cave to keep merchandise in? Will you wait for me a moment?"

"I'm leaving."

"Wait for me a moment."

He went out waving his hand slowly, insisting that Correa wait for him, and then locked the door.

The simple fact that he was locked up frightened Correa more than the argument he had had with the bullies (he explained: "I wasn't expecting anything when they beat me up"). He could hear, although he couldn't make out the words, that the man was talking on the telephone, in the next room. They're not going to get me into trouble, he thought. I'm going out the window. The window faced onto a dark garden; its iron bars were very close together. He could always cry for help, with the risk that the man would hear him before anybody else, and . . . Better not to think about it.

The gentleman's "moment" lasted a long half-hour. Then Correa heard the key turning in the lock, and saw the door opening and the man entering, followed by the two bullies. That night's terrors would never end.

"Here we are, all together again," said the shorter man. "For the good of everybody concerned, I would like to think."

"In that cave of yours, there must be a lot of merchandise, right?" the big man asked with sincere interest.

"It's not a cave, and there's absolutely nothing there."

The man with the white mustache said: "Watch what you say."

"What do you want me to do? Make up stories?"

The man said: "There's no harm in taking a look."

"That's right," the shorter man warned Correa. "For your personal well-being we'd better find the cave nice and full."

"Who's going to find it?" Correa asked, without getting alarmed.

"You. You're joining us on the pleasure cruise, and we're appointing you captain," the big man said gaily.

"I'm not sure I'll find it."

"Now you're starting in with that?"

"The doctor took me there only once. I'm new in the area. All the places along the coast look the same to me."

"There's no harm in trying," the moustachioed man said. "But you two, don't flatten him out again. With that hoodlum stuff we'll never get anywhere. If I hadn't butted in, what would we have known about the cave?"

They put Correa in a car, in the backseat. On one side was the big man, on the other the fat one. The man with the white moustache drove. Dawn was coming when they reached the coast.

Correa became sad and, unable to hold himself back, said: "I'm sure that I'm not going to recognize the island and that you're going to kill me. I prefer that you kill me now."

The two bullies received those words with smiles. The other man explained to them: "For him, it's no laughing matter. He comes from the provinces and doesn't like to be thrown into the water."

They took off in the boat. The fat man was at the helm, talking to the big one; Correa and the other man sat farther back. Correa was very frightened, very sad, and stiff with cold. The cuts on his face were smarting and his body ached. Without knowing why, he fixed his attention on a rowboat that was in tow and on two oars lying on the top of the boat.

When they reached Encarnación, the man said: "Here's where we get off."

With surprising agility Correa stood up. The others started to laugh.

The fat man said to him: "Don't get your hopes up, we're going to be sailing for a while. The gentleman was only remembering that we got off here that night you traveled with your buddy the doctor."

The moustachioed man said to the big man: "You went asleep right away, didn't you?"

"I didn't mean to."

"We're not talking about that. Answer my question."

"Around this part of the coast I was still awake, but I started fighting off sleep then, which was a nuisance."

"You did great." He stared at Correa and asked: "Did you two change boats at any time?"

"No, why?"

"How long did you travel downstream before you got off at the island?"

"Twenty minutes at least. A half-hour, who knows. The island's on the right."

"Keep your eyes wide open—if you try hard, you'll find it."

Correa asserted: "My motto has always been 'Seek and

ye shall find.'" He wondered if he hadn't said the wrong thing.

"That's the spirit," the man exclaimed, and patted him on the back.

Correa thought that perhaps destiny was offering him his best opportunity. It seemed highly improbable that he would find the island on his own, and apparently he couldn't count on the doctor anymore. Now these men were forcing him to find it. The tunnel would take him to Punta del Este in a jiffy, and he would take advantage of the general confusion to escape. No force in the world would prevent him from being reunited with Cecilia.

He said to himself that perhaps he hadn't faithfully kept the tunnel a secret, as he had promised, but he acted under the threat of death and because he could not harm the doctor anymore.

In the calm of that uneventful, smooth river voyage, Correa dozed off until the river entered a wider, more open area where the colors were lighter. On the left bank appeared a sawmill, and on the right a plantation of poplars in endless rows. Then, but not immediately, Correa was startled. Although he was incapable of recognizing any place along the coast, he knew that he had never seen this one before. Frightened, he murmured: "I think we went too far."

The big man stood up, unhurriedly finished his conversation with his fat friend, walked over to Correa, and slapped him twice.

"Enough," the man with the mustache ordered. "Let's turn around." He turned to Correa and said: "You keep your eyes peeled."

Correa's face smarted, and he wondered if he should tell those gangsters exactly what he thought, without worrying about the consequences. When he finally spoke, he thought he was complaining like a child. "If we're going by in the opposite direction, I'll be totally confused."

"You try a man's patience!" the man remarked.

Afterward—a half-hour must have passed—Correa managed to calm down and answer: "I'd like to see you feel the way I feel, with the threat of more beatings hanging over me. I think I'm completely rattled; if not, I would have found the island already. In the direction we were going, it was on the right bank; it has a rotting wooden dock which at some point must have been painted green . . ."

"I'm thinking about what happened to you with us," the man said. "Since everybody lies in this world, we don't believe anything, and when someone comes along who's telling the truth, we teach him a lesson. I believe you."

Correa continued his description: "If you look in a straight line from the dock toward the end of the island, you'll see, almost covered by the trees, a little wooden house. If you walk about fifty yards to the left and go into an area where the trees and bushes are thickest, you'll find the mouth of the tunnel. Remember what I'm telling you: It's not a cave, it's a tunnel."

The gentleman told the bullies: "Now since this young man must be tired, we should leave him at his house."

"First he has to take us to the cave," said the fat man.

The man reminded him: "People who keep their mouths shut don't make mistakes." To Correa he said: "We'll leave you alone, but can we count on your discretion, or are you going to kick this around all over the place?"

"I'm not going to talk."

They knew where he was staying: they took him straight to Mercader's island. To moor the boat, the big man stuck an oar down to the bottom of the river. Finding it hard to believe that those people were letting him go free, Correa jumped to the dock. At that moment, suddenly ashamed of himself, he remembered Cecilia, and he wanted to tell the man that he would go with them, that he would help them find the tunnel. When he turned around to speak, he managed to see a smile on the man's face and, very close, wet, shining, and large, the oar. He fell down onto the muddy grass the same instant it hit him, hard. The blow was very heavy, but not terrible, because he saw it coming and bent over backward. He didn't lose consciousness, but he remained still, just in case. When he no longer heard the motor, he looked. He got up, went into the house, gathered his things, took the first ferry to El Tigre and the first train to Buenos Aires. He wanted to continue to his native province, to feel protected and at home, but he stayed in Buenos Aires, with the intention of returning to Uruguay, whenever he could put together the money for the trip, because he really believed he couldn't live without Cecilia.

Mercader, to whom he went for a loan, told him: "You're forgetting that Perón's government has forbidden travel to Uruguay. Perhaps we could go to El Tigre and talk to a boatman, one of those who take political refugees, or to a smuggler."

Correa said: "We'd better not." Nor did he go looking for the tunnel. He didn't need to see it to know that it existed. As for communicating his knowledge to others, it seemed a useless effort. In due time he got his law degree, and because everything happens sooner or later, retired as a civil servant. A man little given to adventure, with an even though melancholy temperament, he would, according to his friends, get excited only in conversations touching on geographical matters. Then Correa, more than once, would show that he was irritable and proud.

Translated by Suzanne Jill Levine

Letter from Punta del Este

Rodolfo Rabanal

THIS YEAR the Russians arrived in Punta del Este, speaking deplorable French. They showed up at the season's end, during the dog days of February. There were fifteen of them, seven women dressed like ladies out of the fifties, and eight men looking like disoriented apparatchiks. I knew they had come with the express purpose of evaluating Punta's potential for tourism, with an eye

RODOLFO RABANAL (1940–) A native of Buenos Aires, Rabanal currently resides in Punta del Este, Uruguay, where he wrote this story in 2006. A journalist by profession, he still contributes actively to some of Argentina's leading newspapers such as *La Nación*, *Clarín*, and *Página 12*. He has received many national and international awards and recognitions including a Fulbright grant in 1979. In 1988 he was awarded a Guggenheim Fellowship for the completion of his novel *La vida brillante*. Rabanal's credits include nine novels, several collections of stories, and a book of essays and chronicles titled *La costa bárbara: Literatura y experiencia* (2000). His latest novel, *La vida privada* will be published this year by Seix Barral.

toward future investments. None of them, I must admit, evoked a Chekhovian sensibility but rather the flagrant prosperity of vulgar Mafiosi, whose fingers are faster than their brains. I don't know whether any deals were struck, but the Russians swore to return. Many Europeans—mainly non-Russians—swear to return, perhaps vindicating, in their way, that Spaniard who discovered the Río de la Plata, believing it was the route to gold.

Indeed the morning of February 20, 1516, was sultry, unremarkable and calm, a perfect morning for Juan Díaz Solís to drop anchor in the deep-water cove at Gorriti Island. Here his men cudgeled wild rabbits and replenished their supply of fresh water. This event makes it plausible to attribute to the Sevillan sea captain—not irrefutably let me add—the inevitable discovery of Punta del Este, whose rocky tip had to be skirted and whose oblong shield-like shape a bare mile away was in constant view. There is no evidence, however, that Solís set foot on a peninsula—Punta del Este was by no means seductive then—nor did he have any intentions of establishing a fort there. Instead, as everyone knows, he chose to sail up Río de la Plata until hungry Charrúa cannibals brought to a brutal end his quest for gold.

For centuries after this "journey of no return" Punta del Este would remain shrouded in a scattered silence of low-lying settlements, usually four or five huts each, inhabited by fishermen living in the wild, runaway African blacks, a few Portuguese deserters, and a handful of elusive gauchos, who resembled feral Andalusians in exile, or Bedouins who had lost their camels. Things did not pick up until the English invaders arrived in 1806. They fared as badly as Solís, and some soldiers fled like rabbits into the wilderness. Hence, to this day, two hundred years later, one finds among the denizens aloof *paisanos* surnamed Harris or Lighton—why, they don't know. I know one, a carpenter by the name of Laiton.

Finally, Punta became a chimera, a vicarious thrill to late Victorian Uruguayans and Argentines. One afternoon in 1952, amidst the sterile amusements of an international film festival, Joan Fontaine and Gérard Philipe became entangled in a twenty-day idyll. And an eighteen-year-old Russian beauty with Mongolian cheekbones and ice green eyes appeared in a two-piece swimsuit so scanty that a wave left her naked on the beach. Her name was Marina Vlady, and at the time a bartender invented a mixed drink in her honor. Fortunately for her, the Charrúa Indians were long gone.

In the last five years, the voyage from Europe to Punta has gained popularity. Marcelino Arriaga, a Basque from Bilbao who opened a resort hotel in José Ignacio, the place to be at the height of the season, has told me that Europeans come upon its shores like Columbus discovering America. Two of these recent "explorers" are the English novelist Martin Amis and the French actress Dominique Sanda. Encased in an arrogant timidity, Amis keeps to himself; Dominique, however, has become a friend.

In point of fact, Punta del Este is a rocky tongue of land a scant twenty blocks long and six or seven wide. Many want to see it as a rural version of Manhattan without taking into account (all pretensions aside) that Manhattan is an island and Punta del Este a peninsula. Main

street, that is *Avenida Gorlero*, is the backbone of this narrow spit which, not without a certain old-style glamour,
curves to its land's end with a lighthouse and, nearby, a
fishermen's chapel. Punta del Este is surrounded on three
sides by the Atlantic and the Cape of Santa María; its tip
is possibly the easternmost point in the Southern Cone.
The Cape, in turn, points implacably, pensively, and stub-
bornly south to the route followed by whales heading to
mate in the distant waters of Patagonia.

Vacationers snarl its peninsular streets in the summertime. But in winter, buildings loom vacant as if on the
heels of an atomic alert, while scavenging seagulls and
black cormorants that nest in mussel-filled crannies walk
the streets. And when the southeasterlies hit, cascading
breakers momentarily obliterate the boardwalk. At times
like these, living in Punta is like living on the high seas.
Even flights from Buenos Aires, 350 kilometers to the
west on the other side of the Río de la Plata, are cancelled,
which means Argentine newspapers are unavailable—in
itself a blessing in disguise if one rules out the Internet.

When the storm blows over and a thickening fog
descends, enveloping the peninsular mini-city in cotton-
wool, all one can make out is the bluish halo that eerily
appears atop the Hotel Casino Conrad, itself a hallucina-
tory cross between Gotham City and Las Vegas and the
place where Brazilian millionaires lose fortunes, and on
occasion their life by their own hand. After dropping $4
million at the casino's hard-driving poker table one Saturday night two years ago, a pudgy Rio de Janeiro business-
man suffering from high blood pressure, Fábio de Alme-
dia, went to bed with a bottle of gin and never woke up.

And three years ago a beautiful naughty girl from São Paolo was thrown out of a fifteenth floor window by her husband after he surprised her in bed with her lover. The image of a woman flying through space like a bird with hair streaming behind, snapped by a young amateur photographer, won an extravagant photo contest sponsored by the local municipality and the Chamber of Commerce. The young man collected the prize money, and the police sequestered the photo as evidence for the court case— also for the peace and prosperity of the hotel in question. Curiously enough, both the husband and the lover, possibly accomplices, vanished into thin air. But people still speak of the woman who flew like a bird for a brief moment captured on film for all eternity.

For conceptual convenience the name of Punta del Este has been extended to include a large part of the seacoast corresponding to the county of Maldonado. So people give Punta del Este as their destination when they are actually going to Punta Ballena, La Barra, Laguna del Sauce, Laguna Blanca, or José Ignacio. And although urbanistically undistinguished, the city of Maldonado is itself famous for being the temporary residence of Charles Darwin in the nineteenth century, and later on, Captain Sir Richard Francis Burton. In *The Voyage of the Beagle*, Darwin, who lived across the street from the cathedral, described how the mixture of saline and alkaline substances in the estuary—formed when the Río de la Plata meets the Atlantic—foments electric storms. The only thing that caught the eye of Sir Richard Burton, the famous translator of *One Thousand and One Nights* and

The Kama Sutra, were taciturn gauchos who lived on stale bread and beef jerky, and beautiful native girls with complexions as pale as the moon. It's only fair to say that neither Darwin nor Burton went into detail. Darwin continued on to Brazil from Maldonado, and Burton had been expressly commissioned by Queen Victoria to spy on the military during the War of the Triple Alliance in Paraguay. That this bleak inaccessible wasteland would one day become an international playground was, at the time, inconceivable.

Maldonado and Punta del Este are so different that the mere ten kilometers separating them seem a thousand. Located in Maldonado Bay at the mouth of the Río de la Plata, the former is alluvial and transitory, a bedroom community for working people from the impoverished interior of the country, people who politicians catered to at election time. Fernandines, as residents of the city are known—its full name is San Fernando de Maldonado— know that their livelihood depends on Punta del Este, a place they regard, on the other hand, as fatuous and pretentious, two moral qualities they unhesitatingly attribute to the Argentines who vacation and live there, especially those from the port city of Buenos Aires. As is often true in such cases, they are both right and wrong, and by splitting the difference "reasonable" coexistence is obtained. Uruguay is a democratic country at heart.

Whenever I go to Maldonado, I visit Mr. Grossi's bookstore on Ituzaingó Street. Grossi has a respectable number of fine rare books and first editions. Among well-guarded collectors' items, he is especially proud of a first edition of Baudelaire's translation of Edgar Allan Poe's tales that includes the famous prologue defining the short story as a literary genre of Modernity. The asking price for the book—numbered, with a partridge-wing silk hard cover—is $500, which no one yet has deigned to pay. Incredulously Grossi maligns his lot of being obliged to live among vocational illiterates, loudmouthed ignoramuses, and unrepentant tightwads. Some years ago I bought an edition of *Les Liasons Dangereuses* edited by Alphonse Lemerre in 1921 in order not to figure on his black list. There is no guarantee, however, that I have been successful. Short and stocky with a round red face, Grossi moves slowly and talks with the clipped precision of an old-fashioned school teacher who adores sarcasm, swears by God he doesn't believe in God, and quotes Voltaire every other day. But above all else, he drinks like a fish. He opens the bookstore each morning at ten and serves himself his first whiskey at eleven. From then on he waits on customers with hooded eyes as if asleep, and perhaps he is. Four shaggy dogs, useful in winter but unbearable in summer, keep him company, along with a faded old *criollo* who drinks *yerba mate* in silence all day long. Grossi, with his categorical ways and opinions, was my first chance acquaintance when I left Buenos Aires for Punta del Este seven years ago.

Except for cases of obligatory expatriation—a habit that became tradition in these parts—we never really know why we change our place of residence. And paradoxically enough, every compulsive traveler is seeking a fixed residence, whether ideal or concrete is beside the point. Before coming to live in Punta del Este, my wife and I visited Portugal, Tuscany, Liguria, Granada, and Provence, imagining the house where we'd deposit our books and raise a dog. I even fantasized about living in the hilly region of the Argentine province of Córdoba. But the choice fell to the Uruguayan coast just across the water. It then became necessary to quickly marshal certain tribal myths in order to validate and internally authorize the selection: Rafael Alberti lived here in a house he called La Gallarda, I said to myself; Astor Piazzolla took refuge here when he felt unloved in Buenos Aires; Jules Supervielle, Jules Laforgue, and Count Lautréamont, I reeled off, were all born in Uruguay, and Borges spent his childhood summers here on an elegant estate in the del Prado district of Montevideo. Buttressed by such symbolic material, I felt heraldically shielded enough to justify the move—in itself indefensible as all whimsical choices are—and to relax.

I suspect that none of us living here year round today— a disparate colony of mainly foreigners—has abandoned the fantasy of traveling in search of some unknown place we imagine as better for being different. My friend and translator Norman Thomas Di Giovanni writes from London asking me what the hell I'm doing here at the ends of the earth. Seen from London, this dot at the southern end of the continent must evoke the fascination of a lost horizon. I then make my correspondent's fascination my own, and experience what I left Buenos Aires for as truly "faraway"—a distortion, I must admit, that I find exciting.

In any event, I never imagined this place would captivate me as it has. It is not easy for me to ascertain the particular magic it works on my spirit, but it may have something to do with a tenuous negative quality that I would call "courteous exclusion" in an atmosphere of casual tolerance. Whatever it is, the effect is liberating in that the place makes few if any demands. The landscape sometimes seems as obvious as a vacation postcard: disconnected, uninhabited, pleasant. Almost the other side of the coin, one might say, from the ferocious vigor of Iguazú Falls, the commanding upsurge of the Andes, or the lakes and forests in Bariloche, disproportionate muscle flexing on the part of nature that takes our breath away. Here what is interesting is small scale but not negligible. Something similar could be said of the peninsula's diffuse spirituality. In the absence of a central essence, no cultural dimension per se stands out in these parts, nor does a secret or concealed dimension induce us to sniff around corners. Over the door of his house in the woods adjoining the Club del Lago, a Hungarian friend has hung a nihilistic inscription that is both jest and metaphysical snare: "In this same place on January 24, 1876, absolutely nothing happened."

But in the months of January and February, the above-mentioned "nothing" decamps into the depths of its Heideggerian cave. Argentines arrive en masse, Brazilians, to a lesser extent, and, on an even smaller scale, tourists from Europe or mostly from the northern hemisphere who come to buy lots for their second (or third) home at the ends of the earth. Beaches instantly overflow with sunbathers, restaurant waiting lists become impossibly long, and loud music can be heard until after sunrise. And naturally, life becomes unbearable. Too much glamour, too much dissipation, too many Audis, Alfa Romeos, Mercedes, and Volvos. Drunk on beer, golden girl nymphets from all climes vomit in the street and smoke joints at all hours of the day and night. For them—and their masculine counterparts—summer in Punta is a high voltage coming-of-age ritual. Brand names everywhere you turn: everyone looks as if they have been dressed by Tommy Hilfiger, and before binging undoes them, everyone smells of Givenchy Amarige, or at least Escape by Calvin Klein. And they themselves—voracious protagonists of the dawn—resemble figures on the movie marquees and ad posters lining streets and highways. With oracular certainty, one slogan affirms "anything is possible." For the credulous this is an article of blind faith.

The two or three big fashion shows of the season—skimpy underwear, flashy hairdos and swimsuits—turn open-air catwalks into a veritable Olympics of sexual exhibitionism. Then come lavish fireworks, costing millions. They drive the dogs crazy, lighting up the revelry with star-bright flashes and deafening bomb blasts that could be announcing the party of the century or the end of the world. Taking tenacious advantage of the pandemonium, commercial greed sends prices sky high for the purpose of financing the following ten months of doing nothing. Some enterprises succeed and others go under. Personally, whenever I can, I escape to Buenos Aires, which is correspondingly empty and consequently humanized by default during these months.

But when the last tourists finally go home, Punta del Este, cleansed as if swept by a wind of bleach, becomes another place, even mysterious. It is as if, driven by the empty coastline, the sudden silence has fanned out over the countryside. An invisible yet efficient vacuum cleaner sucks up the summertime hullabaloo in a matter of hours, extending a serenity akin to oblivion over what was a madhouse a short time before. Even stores that advertised "everything for sale except the staff" pack up and disappear from one day to the next, some without even bothering to pay the two-month rental fee. Left on the sand are trembling green jellyfish, a poisonous gelatin medallion with violet pseudopods that we call "living water." And those of us who are left behind are the members of what might be called the "permanent cast."

Until recently Juan Patricio Walcot was a member of this cast. In September 2003 he made me a gift of his Patagonian poems, along with a bottle of Italian grappa. The book, which he had printed himself, is exquisitely illustrated with his own watercolor landscapes. The poems are austere and dispassionate. The first poem in the book describes the moment before an animal is butchered:

> *In the water, beneath the cliffs,*
> *a black-necked swan*
> *is ready for death.*
> *Above the hill, in the sky, a gray falcon*
> *circles down.*

Walcot was born in Patagonia; his parents were English and he was educated in England and the United States, where he specialized in aviation engines. An experienced pilot at the age of 20, he enlisted in the Air Force and flew a fighter-bomber in Korea. After the war he set up a private air taxi service, married a rich Argentine, and bred livestock in the province of Buenos Aires.

One day he decided he wanted to be Uruguayan, crossed the river, bought thirty acres in Laguna Blanca, and built a colonial-style house with a long gallery of columns and up above, a widow's walk. Divorced from his first wife, he lost no time and quickly married María. A Chilean of Mapuche descent, María was stockily built with the features of a nocturnal idol. A peculiarity of hers, perhaps the only one aside from her aboriginal economy of expression, is to climb trees like a monkey. From up in the branches she sings and calls to Juan Patricio. But he detests heights, despite—or possibly because of—his past as a pilot. According to the apparently well-informed grapevine, María was his housekeeper while he was sick, and thus earned a place for herself as his companion and guardian angel. This may very well be true. A woman of few words, María takes care of the house and nods hello to visitors. Juan Patricio attends social gatherings without her. María got pregnant in 2004; Juan Patricio, immersed in his poems, appeared elusive and unhappy. One winter night, while crossing the suspension bridge connecting La Barra with Punta del Este, the car he was driving swerved inexplicably and fell into the river. María dove twice, got her husband out of the car, and swam to shore with him, thus saving his life. I cross this bridge at least twice a day and still can't understand how the car went off the bridge into the water. Again according to local gossip, the couple was having a fight; indeed, serious scandalmongers insist he wanted to kill her, only to be countered by others saying it was the other way around. Last year Juan Patricio Walcot fell gravely ill and died soon after. María, the Mapuche who climbs trees, is now the sole owner of the colonial house where she is raising young Walcot, whose existence Juan Patricio barely acknowledged.

Walcot was one of the "winter residents," meaning he lived here all year round, not a vacationer or even a home-owner from Buenos Aires who visits Punta at least once a month and claims to feel "perfectly at home." Laguna Blanca, where this benevolent Anglo-Argentine, who dropped thousands of bombs on Korea and wrote terse poems, lived, happens to be around three kilometers from my house in a wooded area 800 meters from the beach at La Barra, and 10 kilometers from where the foothills begin, which means that, for all practical purposes, I live in the country—something that scandalized Norman Thomas Di Giovanni even more—and I have a neighbor who runs a modest dairy consisting of two milk cows and a calf. I've said nothing about this neighbor to Norman. But I have mentioned the Old Man.

When March comes and the now-empty beaches are ours once again, there is nothing more pleasant than visiting *Parada* 30 on the Atlantic, where there is a rustic "eating place" made of wood planks topped by a reed roof. On the wide terrace out front is a brick barbecue, and the Old Man, of course, reigns supreme. The Old Man lives year round in this shack accompanied by a bevy of old Labradors too lazy to bark. In summer he barbecues meat and fish for townspeople, but come March he only does it for his friends. I usually bring over a kilo of smelt filets and a bottle of red wine. If the day is warm I go for a swim while he barbecues the fish. On other occasions I go down to the beach in late afternoon to gaze at the sea and the famous *Isla de Los Lobos* about 18 miles offshore. Then the Old Man asks me what I'm looking at, and I tell him that, looking straight ahead, I can see Tasmania outlined on the other side of the world. Nodding resignedly, he gives me a toothless smile. This generic appellative, the Old Man's only name, defines him: a man who has always been old. A fisherman by profession, now retired, his face is so wrinkled and weather-beaten that it is a bit difficult to distinguish his features. He always wears the same clothes, except in winter when he wraps himself in an old waterproof deep-sea fisherman's jacket and dons a visorless wool cap. He then looks like a beach bum, which is essentially what he is. On cool afternoons he prefers a glass of whiskey, accompanied by cubes of sharp *Colonia* cheese, slices of "homemade" salami, and a round loaf of country bread. I join him for a glass of whiskey quite often, the two of us looking out over the changing expanse of the ocean and the empty beach. For decades Uruguay was unable to make decent wine, so Uruguayans became fond of whiskey. They produce good wine now but still don't dare give up whiskey. With the Old Man, especially if there is whiskey, conversation consists more of silences than words, the latter often monosyllables or isolated nouns bereft of adjectives. When I think about this man, the elemental solitude surrounding us comes alive, just as if the pampa, transformed into a spiritual category, has infiltrated our soul, causing horizontal vertigo. At such times the mundane concept of Punta del Este becomes immaterial, its summertime video clip contours dissolving to form a faded picture speaking to us of something alien.

When we are alone at last, between the end of summer and the amber threshold of fall, I may even ask myself, not without a certain neophytic perplexity, just what I am doing here and how did I land in such a godforsaken place, with so many other places to be, in this wide world. The question is, of course, superfluous because it rules out any reasonable answer: rather, it is a spiritual game posing a chimerical challenge played at day's end when the white owl begins its unfathomable comments on the fleetingness of things. Not unlike the game that arises when the Old Man asks me to explain "where Tasmania falls" and I explain it to him by drawing a map with the tip of my finger in the dust on the table; he then says: "Those people are really far away . . ."

"And us?" I ask him.

Baffled, he looks at me and responds: "We are here."

Translated by Suzanne Jill Levine

The Boundless River

Juan José Saer

TWO OR THREE FRIENDS are waiting at the airport when I arrive, and after the formalities of customs and greetings, we undertake the car ride from the airport into the city. My trips home almost always take place around the same time of year, and so the same clear spring morning, under a blue sky in which not a single cloud can be seen, sparkles in the deserted plain that extends from either edge of the road to the horizon. Many of the numerous travelers who have written about the Río de la Plata region coincide in two, apparently contradictory

---

JUAN JOSÉ SAER (1937–2005) Considered by some to be one of the best writers of the 20th century, Saer, originally from the province of Santa Fe, moved to Paris in 1968 where he enjoyed a prolific literary career. His background in cinematography had a strong visual impact on his writings. A predominant theme in his work is that of exile. The fragment included here from *El río sin orillas* (1991), literally "the river without banks," celebrates both the expansiveness of the River Plate as well as the richness of Argentine culture.

observations: the delicious clemency of its climate, and the frequent occurrence of storms. Both are absolutely true, as I have had the opportunity to confirm in a single sojourn, and even in a single afternoon. After half an hour on the road from the airport, we arrived in the lovely neighborhood of Caballito, an area which in the first decades of the last century was occupied by cooperatives, Socialists, and Utopians, at the house of my friends Juan Pablo Renzi and María Teresa Gramuglio, who for years have housed me during my stays in Buenos Aires. They are both from Rosario, but in 1975, repeated threats from paramilitary groups forced them to lose themselves in the capital, until they eventually found anchor in that magical house filled with the canvases of Renzi and other Argentine painters. Friends start to drop in, while the *asado* crackles in the patio. And the day goes by in polemics, jokes, stories, and games, until the evening when, exhausted, Juan Pablo, María Teresa, and I sit down to watch a movie on television, a final touch of irresponsibility to supplement our fatigue and complete the abandonment of all critical self-control which then allows us to give in to sleep.

I must note that, when I informed them of my project (to write a book about the Río de la Plata), many of my friends felt obligated to supply me with leads, information, and theories that, in their opinion, were "indispensable" to its success. The night before, in mid-flight, a friend who happened to be on the plane with me warned me darkly: "Did you know that the surface of the Río de la Plata (34,000 square kilometers) is equal to that of Holland?" My friend perceived a challenge in the very size of the river, as if I were not about to *write* about the estuary, but rather to swim across it. In Buenos Aires, during the welcome party, several guests presented me with anecdotes, references, and theories, as one would present useful tools to a traveler who is about to set out on a long, difficult voyage. And in the same way that, masking his discouragement with good manners, the traveler observes the accumulation in his luggage of useless objects that he had decided to do without and which he will now have to lug with him during the entire voyage, I listened to this accumulation of pertinent details regarding my subject, and came to the realization that just as with every object in this world, and even with the world as an object, there are as many Ríos de la Plata as there are tales of the river itself. In this case, Heraclitus's notion that you can never step into the same river twice, and the even more radical variant by one of his disciples—you cannot step into the same river even once—might admit a more particular variation: as in a dream, each person tries, unsuccessfully, to step into his own river.

Yes; the Arabs call the young palm tree al-yatit, al-wadi, al-hira, al-fasil, al-asa, al-kafur, al-damd, and al-igrid; when the date appears they call it al-sayad, and when it turns green, before it becomes hard, they call it al yadal; when it grows large, they call it al-busr; when the skin becomes grooved they call it al-mujattam; when its color changes from green to reddish, they call it suqja; when it turns completely red, it becomes al-zahw; when it begins to ripen and to be covered in spots it becomes busra muwakketa; when it is time to harvest it, it becomes al-inad; when the peduncle begins to darken it becomes mudanniba; when half of it is ripe, it has two names: al-mujarra and al-muyazza; when two thirds are ripe it becomes hulqana, and when it is completely ripe, it is called munsabita.

This is just a small sample, a single drop from our oceans, adds the poet Ibn Burd, compounding his boastfulness. Many words to name the same thing, or a specific word for each of the infinite aspects of the infinity of things, such are the difficulties that arise in the act of writing, difficulties which some, with unexpected childishness, like Ibn Burd, take pride in.

In this sense, the River, despite its geographical vastness, with its profusion of twists and events, is more vast and unapproachable not only than Holland, but than the entire universe. Its history, dark and marginal in comparison with the great accomplishments of the Orient and the Occident, teems with heroes, wise men, and tyrants. In the abstract geography of the plain, in the infinite emptiness of the desert, certain human acts, individual or collective, certain fugitive presences, have acquired the massive permanence of the pyramids and the cathedrals of Europe. And if these acts seem to float, light in the transparent air of the plain, revealing its mirage-like quality, we must not forget that, from a certain point of view, cathedrals and pyramids are no different.

Be that as it may, the day after my arrival, I began in earnest my campaign to gather the indispensable materials for my task. In accordance with one of the two invariable and contradictory observations of the many travelers who have come to this part of the world, it was a glorious morning, sunny, warm, and without a cloud in the entire sky which, as is well known, is more visible in the plain than in areas with more varied terrain. In the taxi that bore me toward the city center, the morning clamor of Buenos Aires increased as we approached the downtown area, down long tree-lined avenues, with the windows open and the radio blaring, and I began to bask in a feeling of identity and belonging which little by little, as in every trip home, began to corrode the intolerable memories and disappointments. The neighborhood of Caballito, half an hour from downtown, on the Avenida Rivadavia, *the longest avenue in the world,* as the Argentines never cease to remind us whenever they can, perhaps in order to console themselves with this record—which can be ascribed to chance rather than to the merit of any one person—for their many diffuse and tenacious doubts and frustrations.

The only urbanistic harmony of Buenos Aires lies in the fact that, like most of the cities in the Americas, it is set on a grid, and that for this reason its straight streets, interrupted every hundred meters, carry on—even if sometimes their names change at the intersection with an avenue—without any curves from where one stands until they are lost in the horizon. The rest of the urban cityscape is typified by variety and whim, and, why not say it, chaos. In its architecture, what attracts the eye is the surprising and the unexpected. The gray uniformity of Paris, on the other hand, offers up to the viewer structures that are balanced by a stylistic will, regulated by the coexistence of different periods of architecture. Even the more recent exceptions to this uniformity (I am not speaking of the marginal neighborhoods that resulted from the real estate speculation of the sixties and seventies) are calculated: the Eiffel Tower, the Plateau Beaubourg, and the Pyramid of the Louvre; they are the result of an intentional break that however bears a certain affinity, formal or conceptual, to the whole to which they stand in opposition. Thus, the Pyramid evokes the obelisk at the Place de la Concorde and the Egyptian collection in the museum itself; and the Plateau Beaubourg, in spite of the iconoclastic nature of its materials, and the bright colors of its external surface which stands out against the generalized gray, tamely acquiesces to the surrounding norms in its proportions. In Buenos Aires, incongruity is the norm. On each block, heterogeneous structures, raised, or maintained, by the economic means, the manual dexterity, the aesthetics, and even the whimsy of their proprietors, coexist. A twenty-story building rises up, improbably stable, next to a modest house with a small front garden, which has been needing a paint job since the forties, and this house in turn shares a dividing wall with a two- or three-story house built at the turn of the century, judging from the niches, angels, and moldings that crowd its façade. Even in the middle of downtown, though to a lesser degree, architectural anarchy is the norm. The straightness of the streets is the only rigor that contains this vertiginous variety, as a square mold holds in an amorphous substance. And if, to be generous, the whole lacks interest, its details surprise, delight, and even dazzle at each step.

Because of this, the traveler, admiring the view from the back seat of a car, or from a bus, cannot abandon himself to the peaceful contemplation of an urban landscape gliding by, but rather, his attention is attracted by many sudden, isolated, successive, or even simultaneous appeals, and he is constantly forced to turn his head, shift from one window to another, or try to fix, in a last glance through the rear window, a fragmentary image—a figure, a façade, a garden—an apparition which, unforeseen and fleeting, the city has offered up and yanked away almost at the same moment.

That morning, my intention was to drive beyond the city center in order to inaugurate my stay with a visit to the river; descending the Avenida Belgrano, the taxi turned north onto the Avenida 9 de Julio. This avenue deserves a brief stop (metaphysical of course, because the taxi is held back only by the traffic lights and the occasional traffic jam) in order to consider it, not so much as an urbanistic accomplishment, but as a symptom: just as the Avenida Rivadavia is the longest avenue in the world, the 9 de Julio is *the widest avenue in the world*. That it is wide is undeniable; that it is the widest in the world could, even without comparative points of reference, be accepted as plausible; but the fact that even the most resentful resident of the provinces, angry at the hegemony of Buenos Aires over the rest of the country, cannot name it without adding with provocative pride that it is *the widest in the world*, reveals a tendency to exalt the insignificant which might be ascribable to an unconscious belief in the painful absence of the truly exalting. The giant cement obelisk which adorns the intersection of the 9 de Julio with the Avenida Corrientes is not to me its principal attraction, but rather the *palos borrachos* (choricia speciosa) with their swollen, spiny pale green trunks. This is a tree whose flowering pattern I have not yet been able to deduce from direct observation, as I have seen specimens blooming at different times of year, alongside their completely bare brethren, as if there were such a thing as individualism in the vegetable kingdom. This observation is confirmed by an earlier jotting in my notebook: "April 4th, Avenida 9 de Julio at 11:45. In a taxi. *Palos borrachos* in bloom (pink, white, ivory). Acacias or *tipas* still quite green."

In the cities of El Litoral—the informed reader should bear with me in this pedagogical aside—in other words, in the provinces along the principal rivers that come together to form the Río de la Plata, three great trees compete for the aesthetic prize when spring rolls around, and they bloom in the following order: the *lapacho,* whose scientific name escapes me, the yellow acacia, common enough in Europe that its Latin name needn't be mentioned, and the *jacarandá,* or *jacaranda mimosifolia.* They successively fill the parks, squares, and avenues with deep pink, yellow, or lilac-colored flowers that cover not only their branches, which often do not even have leaves on them yet, but also and especially the ground beneath them, so that on some narrow, tree-lined streets one walks literally on a carpet of one of these colors, or sometimes of two colors combined, since the acacias and *jacarandás* bloom more or less simultaneously. In Caballito, the enormous acacias on the Calle Pedro Goyena—in my opinion, one of the most beautiful streets in Buenos Aires—lay down a bright yellow covering over the sidewalks and the street for half a kilometer, while the street that crosses it, Del Barco Centenera—the first poet to sing the glory of Argentina—opts, with equal abundance, for the lilac hue of the *jacarandás*. The beauty of this spectacle is so extreme that even the most insensitive beings can perceive it, and in the years of the military dictatorship, from 1975 to 1983—the bloodiest of any of the bloody dictatorships we have endured—the regime's propaganda tried to hide the horrendous crimes it committed every day behind a curtain, not of smoke, but of ephemeral pink, yellow, and lilac-colored flowers, a fact that should remind us that in authoritarian societies, everything can be subjugated. For that reason, an anonymous opposer of the tyranny invented two disparaging neologisms—*lapachiento* and *jacarandoso*—to describe the image of the country that the usurpers in power attempted to exhibit to the outside world.

Translated by Marina Harss

The Blessing

Edgar Brau

OUR PRESIDENTIAL RESIDENCE is situated in the very center of the Capital, and two or three blocks of luxurious mansions surround it like protective rings. Continuing outward from these homes, the humbleness of the outlying dwellings accelerates at an extraordinary pace. At a distance of five blocks they are little more than shacks, and at the periphery, they are miserable hovels.

A geometric garden, dotted here and there with flower beds, encircles the central building—almost a hundred

EDGAR BRAU (1958–) Born in Resistencia, Argentina, in the northern province of Chaco, actor, painter, and photographer, Brau is the author of thirteen collections of poetry and fiction. His work is gradually becoming known in English thanks in part to a grant from the National Endowment for the Arts in 2000 awarded to Donald A. Yates, who with Joanne M. Yates and Andrea Labinger co-translated Brau's *Casablanca and Other Stories* (Michigan State Press, 2006). His newest collection, *Suite Argentina* (*Argentine Suite*) contains four "movements" that pay homage to the victims of the Dirty War.

years old and ornately Italian. For some time now, the
garden has attracted the gazes and murmurings of the
citizens on account of a strange ceremony that unfolds on
its paths each evening. What happens is that as soon as
be finishes his dinner, the President goes into the garden
accompanied by an aide-de-camp who carries a silver
tray with a revolver on it. When they arrive at the head
of the main path, the aide-de-camp presents the tray to
the President, who, in the meantime, has pulled on some
silk gloves. The President takes the gun, examines it,
nods in approval, and then, as he begins strolling around
the grounds, fires it overhead. The pauses between one
discharge and the next are regular, almost exactly timed,
and the President stops only for the aide-de-camp to load
the gun once its chamber has been emptied.

When the first shot rings out, the poorest people go
out onto the patio or porch of their homes and stay there,
waiting expectantly. Those who have children line them
up on a bench and make them sit there. So as not to be
late, the crippled take their places one by one a little early
and ease their wait by quietly reciting certain concilia-
tory prayers. And after a little while, when the shooting
ceases, everyone starts asking who could be the lucky one
who managed to be wounded by the President . . .

And yet, it hasn't been long since the people used to
tremble when the shooting began (which apparently
helped the President to relax and manage a good night's
sleep) and no one dared to go out into the street for fear
of being "blessed by the President's bullet," as they used
to say jokingly. But one night, while her parents were distracted, a little girl went out onto the patio of her home,

curious about the gunshots. After awhile, her mother noticed she was gone and ran out to find her. But it was too late; the little girl was lying on the ground, bleeding. She wasn't dead, however, because the bullet had only struck her in the arm. They were humble people; they carried the girl to a hospital and merely asked that she be helped. But even at that, the word spread until it reached the President himself. So that one fine day an enormous black automobile pulled up in front of the little girl's house, and she and her parents promptly got out of the back seat, smiling and loaded down with packages. The girl's arm was bandaged, but she looked just fine.

Immediately the whole neighborhood converged on the home where the auto was parked. The house was filled to overflowing with friends from the neighborhood and the relatives who had waited for the family's arrival. The girl's mother didn't leave out a single detail in describing the staff's attentions at the luxurious clinic, in explaining the scholarship that the President had awarded her daughter, and in displaying all the gifts. Meanwhile, her husband was telling these astonished visitors about his new job, which was also a part of the compensation for the child's accident. And the presence of the uninformed chauffeur—who smiled as he drank a soda—seemed to make what the bedazzled parents described even more magnificent.

When the automobile left later on, the neighbors departed from the modest house in silence; the grown-ups among them appeared deep in thought. And even though no one said a word, that same night many of the children were obliged to look at the stars in the open air, while underneath their breaths, their parents prayed that they might receive the "blessing" of the President. Then there was a brief suspension in the routine firings: the presidential advisors needed time to persuade their leader to use the people's anticipation of help to political advantage.

Over the months other incidents occurred, some fatal. There were even one or two that were intentionally fraudulent—certain parents purposely wounded their own children—but this stratagem was countered when the President began using bullets specially marked in order to prevent false claims.

Later, when a vagrant was wounded, the category of "Adults" was created, which also necessitated creating an office for investigating the claims of those who somehow felt unfairly treated. Not long afterward, for example, a group of neighbors came forward to denounce certain opportunists who rented their backyards to people living further out and making them pay by the minute for their stay. Aware of the complaint and knowing that sooner or later they would be kicked out, those temporary tenants demanded in turn the use of a revolver with a better range than the one the President was in the habit of using. But to date no word has been released in this regard, although it has been decreed that the children of well-to-do families who are wounded (they compete with each other to expose themselves to the bullets) will not receive any compensation. At the same time, the sale of certain talismans that supposedly attract bullets was prohibited.

Humanitarian organizations had no choice but to make their displeasure known. But, although their reasons are completely worthy of consideration, it is ridiculous to think of suppressing the presidential custom. The people have become so used to it, find so much hope and satisfaction in its existence (the cities outside the capital are now demanding something similar), that it has become a virtual reason of state; perhaps the most important one. So much so, people say, that although apparently moved by the image of wounded people (detractors correct this, saying *his* image communicated to foreign countries is the real concern), the president had once more intended to halt the shootings, but an explicit threat from the Army stopped him. Others say that the President no longer does the shooting, and that some official takes his place; and they add that the President takes advantage of these moments to mingle with the people and share the risks. Those who deny this rumor, talk instead about officials disguised as the president, and about the electoral benefit in future elections. But these are all suppositions. Until now, no one has seen the President or any double in the streets. Indeed, the public even talks openly about their preference for a safe president who shoots off bullets from his garden into the night. So the only thing that continues to be real, night after night, is the existence of a grassy path, traversed by a man who every so often raises his arm and, perhaps with a grimace, fires his gun.

Translated by Joanne M. Yates

Bed Time Story

Ana María Shua

THEN SHE WALKED resolutely, determined but timid, as those days demanded, with a sort of controlled boldness, right into his apartment, and he led her into the bedroom without deliberation, better not to give her time to change her mind, to think of obstacles, her voice becoming a barrier, better to leave it to the silence of their bodies, there, in the bedroom, that damned, haughty, brutal waterbed, one of the first in the country, the pride of its owner, inflated, definitive, forbidden, they fell upon

---

ANA MARÍA SHUA (1951–) Born in Buenos Aires, Ana María Shua is one of the most active contemporary writers. She is at home in a number of genres, but one of her main loves is the short, short story known as *minificción*. The recipient of numerous awards, including a Guggenheim Grant, she has written children's stories, plays, poetry, and fiction. Her work often focuses on Jewish Argentine culture and has been translated into a number of languages and into film. Her stories have recently been re-compiled in the volume *Que tengas una vida interesante* (2009).

it, and as they undressed with the awkward, irrevocable intensity of the first time, she learned, little by little, to mount it, to keep her balance on it, a waterbed requires taming, demands the skill of an accomplished rider, but afterward what bliss, what harmony, what interplay of waves and fluids, and how she learned to enjoy it, that crazy bed, while he learned everything there was to know about her, odors, hairs, that never-routine joining of tongues, and one day, so comfortable they fell asleep together, only to awaken practically on the floor, drenched, surrounded by a lake, laughing, touching, bailing out the water, swearing at the damned punctured plastic, naked, sweeping the water away with driers and buckets and rags and games and the downstairs neighbor complaining about the damp ceiling, their hyperbolic love liquids filtering into the neighbor's apartment, triggering complaints from the other tenants, and they laughed and drained, pursuing the water, pursuing each other. But later it wasn't all games between them anymore, and their caresses went beyond their skin, they caressed each other's lungs and pancreases, it wasn't just their mouths loving anymore, it was their tonsils and their souls, and separation hurt after so much love, and then she began sleeping over more and more often, and the waves became less amusing, pleasant, as wild as ever but not so divine, every time one of them moved in his sleep, the waves rocked the other one, their sleep was fitful, problematic, waking to a punctured mattress and morning obligations was irritating, they wanted to bail out the water and laugh and wring the rags like before, but it was a weekday with schedules, and the world was out there, demanding its

due, they cleaned and dried and decided to buy a real bed,
maybe get married, but not in church, an inexpensive
foam rubber mattress. And then the country itself was
shaken by a waterbed which became a tidal wave, a tide
that threatened to swallow them up, there were persecutions, official and unofficial, someone might come looking for them, it was time to change location, change
houses, it wasn't easy to find anyone willing to take them
in, one night they picked up the new foam rubber mattress, carrying it somehow between the two of them down
patrolled streets, carrying a bed could be a sign of disturbing the peace, of danger, of subversion, a sign of
death. For a few days they slept badly in the borrowed,
shared house, making furtive, forbidden love, like adoles-
cents hiding from their parents, until they had their pass-
ports ready. It was in Paris that they set up the other bed,
a little Paris apartment with a tiny bathroom and an
impossible bed, a sunken-in, broken-down *sommier* and
so little money that finally they thought of turning it
upside down, legs up, mattress lodged between the legs,
army blankets from the flea market, so threadbare and
moth-eaten, and their good Argentine winter coats protecting them from the relentless, boring, long, sad Paris
winter, and after a while the certainty that it wasn't there
that they wanted to have their child, not in that city or in
that bed. Then the return, they went back to that foam
rubber mattress that hadn't been sold, nearly new, and
there, in their forever city, her belly grew so large, she
seemed so fragile and yet so tremendous, so regal, all-
encompassing, dominant, that he got used to sleeping
curled up in a ball, he got used to making himself smaller,

occupying minimal space, a wise habit because before long there would be three of them in that bed, they brought the baby in with them just to nurse but soon all three of them slept there and as soon as she began to walk, those little steps invading at dawn, flip-flop, mother protesting, father hugging, sleeping on his side, lying almost on the bed frame, the tiny, spread-eagled princess happy in the middle of the bed, then they had others, each one in turn figuring out how to occupy the middle of the bed, sleeping meant sharing new smells, of diapers, urine, baby poop, fresh milk, sweat and spit-up, but eventually they also learned that children come and go away, and at last none of them remained. And it should be recognized that at this point they also knew other beds, round ones with canopies, all of them short-sheeted, the violent perfumes of some wayside hotel, other he's for her and other she's for him, and yet they always slept together. They made more money and they moved and they wanted something both of them had dreamed of: a *sommier* like the one in Paris but brand new, with the softest, most comfortable mattress in the world, on top of the *sommier* a mattress with some small springs and other, larger ones, that was their dream and it was fulfilled and for a few years they slept semi-submerged, their still-young bones adjusting to their relative weights, and yet, as the years passed, their pancreases lungs tonsils that had loved each other so and still did, in a way, started wearing out and their back problems began. They gave up the inner-spring mattress, went back to a foam rubber mattress that looked nothing like that first one, it was thicker and, above all, much harder, as hard as some of the woolen mattresses of their respective childhoods, the ones that had to be carded from time to time. But even all that hardness wasn't enough, soon they surrendered, first the *sommier*, then came the bed board under the mattress, backaches, nights were long then, complicated. They no longer slept as they had in their adolescence, nor with the deep desperation of those dreams their children had disturbed, both of them got up, moved around, began waking earlier, at midnight their bladders cried out, urinating became part of the passage of the hours. They struggled mutely now, two individuals of substance, of weight, of a certain age, they fought for vital space, a silent combat, the bed their boxing ring. Every night when they went to bed, they divided the battlefield, prepared their weapons, equitably distributed pillows and blankets, a little more on the side of the one who pulled less, a section of the quilt tucked under the mattress to defend their battle positions. Then he began to talk about separate beds, they visited ordinary furniture stores, maybe two beds, they visited sophisticated furniture stores, connected beds but also separable, with a motor, a little expensive, when suddenly she became gravely ill, and a long hospital stay took her from their bed, he had it to himself all night long and didn't enjoy it, he missed the shoves and elbow pokes, the abrupt movements of sleep, the inconsiderate, brutal way she would plop down again on the mattress, he missed it all, he missed the annoying, embarrassing smells of an aging woman, the touch of loose, slightly saggy flesh, the skin that was no longer so tense in their embraces but still so very hers, their bodies competing and touching, giving each other hate and heat in that bed: he missed it. And so, when she came home, they stopped talking about separate beds, although after a brief cease-fire the nightly combat and annoyance returned, he suffered from acid reflux and the doctor recommended sleeping with his head elevated. Then they discussed whether to saw off the front legs, decided to add supports to elevate the back ones, it would also help his breathing, reducing sleep apnea and snoring, their nights were a concert now, worse if he had a slight cold, sometimes she awoke in the darkness feeling like she was in the middle of a storm, deep, tangled winds, his breathing in her ear, exquisite, desired, and now unbearable: they were old. One night the intolerable noise awoke her again, his deep exhalation, long and practically stentorian but then what a relief silence brought, she could recapture her sweetest sleep, the profound sleep of early morning and she awoke with the strange sensation of absence, something was incomplete, the exasperating sound of air intake was missing, this time there had been no inhalation, and beginning the very next night she was the ruler of the entire bedspace at last, the solitary victor. And so it continued for years, slow, laborious years like those of childhood, her mind growing distant, foggy, only momentarily parting the clouds, the doctor's words that day, near the end, advising, talking to her children at her bedside, in order to avoid those reddish areas that tend to blister, form wounds, bedsores, that voice firmly advising: we'll have to put her in a waterbed.

Translated by Andrea G. Labinger

Return Trip Tango

Julio Cortázar

Le hasard meurtrier se dresse au coin de la première rue.
Au retour l'heure-couteau attend.

Marcel Bélanger, *Nu et noir*

ONE GOES ALONG recounting things ever so slowly, imagining them at first on the basis of Flora or a door opening or a boy who cries out, then that baroque necessity of the intelligence that leads it to fill every hollow until its perfect web has been spun and it can go on to something new. But how can we not say that perhaps, at some time or another, the mental web adjusts itself, thread by

---

JULIO CORTÁZAR (1914–1984) One of the most original writers of the 20th century, Cortázar is best known for his innovations in narrative structure which call upon the reader to be an active participant, as exemplified by his novel *Rayuela* (*Hopscotch*, 1963). He saw writing as having a life of its own once it detached itself from the writer, "like a bubble from a bubble pipe." Born in Brussels of Argentine parents, he eventually chose to leave Argentina in 1951 in the face of Peronism to work as a translator for UNESCO in Paris from where he continued to write and to fight for human rights and the end of dictatorships.

---

thread, to that of life, even though we might be saying so
purely out of fear, because if we didn't believe in it a little,
we couldn't keep on doing it in the face of outside webs.
Flora, then, and she told me everything little by little
when we got together, no longer worked at Miss Matilde's (she still called her that even though she didn't have
any reason now to continue giving her that title of respect
from a maid of all work). I enjoyed having her reminisce
about her past as a country girl from La Rioja who'd come
down to the capital with great frightened eyes and little
breasts that in the end would be worth more in life for her
than any feather duster or good manners. I like to write
for myself, I've got notebooks and notebooks, poetry, and
even a novel, but what I like to do is write, and when I
finish it's like a fellow's slipping aside after the pleasure,
sleep comes, and the next day there are other things rap-
ping on your window, that's what writing is, opening the
shutters and letting them in, one notebook after another:
I work in a hospital, I'm not interested in people reading
what I write, Flora or anybody else; I like it when I finish
a notebook, because it's as if I'd already published it, but
I haven't thought about publishing it, something raps on
the window and we're off again on a new notebook the
way you would call an ambulance. That's why Flora told
me so many things about her life without imagining that
later on I would go over them slowly, between dreams,
and would put some into a notebook. Emilio and Matilde
went into the notebook because it couldn't remain just
Flora's tears and scraps of memory. She never spoke to
me about Emilio and Matilde without crying at the end.
After that I didn't ask her about it for a few days, even

steered her to other memories, and one beautiful morning I led her gently back to that story again, and Flora rushed into it again as if she'd already forgotten everything she'd told me, began all over, and I let her because more than once her memory brought back things she hadn't mentioned before, little bits that fitted into other little bits, and, for my part, I was watching the stitches of the suture appear little by little, the coming together of so many scattered or presumed things, puzzles during insomnia or *mate* time. The day came when it would have been impossible for me to distinguish between what Flora was telling me and what she and I myself had been putting together, because both of us, each in his or her own way, needed, like everybody, to have that business finished, for the last hole finally to receive the piece, the color, the end of a line coming from a leg or a word or a staircase.

Since I'm very conventional, I prefer to grab things from the beginning, and, besides, when I write I see what I'm writing, I really see it, I'm seeing Emilio Díaz on the morning he arrived at Ezeiza airport from Mexico and went down to a hotel on the Calle Cangallo, spent two or three days wandering about among districts and cafés and friends from other days, avoiding certain encounters but not hiding too much either, because at that moment he had nothing to reproach himself for. He was probably slowly studying the terrain in Villa del Parque, walking along Melincué and General Artigas, looking for a cheap hotel or boardinghouse, settling in unhurriedly, drinking *mate* in his room, and going out to a bistro or the movies at night. There was nothing of the ghost about him, but he didn't speak much and not to many people, he walked

on crepe soles and wore a black windbreaker and brown
pants, his eyes quick for the get-up-and-go, something
that the landlady of the boardinghouse would have called
sneakiness; he wasn't a ghost but he looked like one from
the distance, solitude surrounded him like another silence,
like the white bandana around his neck, the smoke of his
butt, never too far away from those almost-too-thin lips.

Matilde saw him for the first time—for this second
first time—from the window of the bedroom on the second floor. Flora was out shopping and had taken Carlitos
along so he wouldn't whimper with boredom at siesta
time, it was the thick heat of January and Matilde was
looking for some air by the window, painting her nails the
way Germán liked them, although Germán was traveling in Catamarca and had taken the car and Matilde was
bored without the car to go downtown or to Belgrano, she
was already used to Germán's absence, but she missed the
car when he took it. He'd promised her another one all
for herself when the firms merged, she didn't understand
those business matters, but evidently they still hadn't
merged, at night she would go to the movies with Perla,
would hire a rental car, they'd dine downtown, afterward
the garage would pass the bill for the car on to Germán,
Carlitos had a rash on his legs and she'd have to take him
to the pediatrician, just the idea made him even hotter,
Carlitos throwing a tantrum, taking advantage of his
father's absence to give her a hard time, incredible how
that kid blackmailed her when Germán was away, only
Flora, with affection and ice cream, Perla and she would
have ice cream too after the movies. She saw him beside a
tree, the streets were empty at that time, under the double

shadow of the foliage that came together up above; the
figure stood out beside a tree trunk, a wisp of smoke
rising up along his face. Matilde drew back, bumping
into an easy chair, muffling a shriek with her hands that
smelled of pink nail polish, taking refuge against the back
wall of the room.

Milo, she thought, if that was thinking, that instan-
taneous vomiting of time and images. It's Milo. When
she was able to look out from another window no one
was on the corner across the way anymore, two children
were coming along in the distance playing with a black
dog. He saw me, Matilde thought. If it was he, he'd seen
her, he was there in order to see her, he was there and not
on any other corner, leaning on any other tree. Of course
he'd seen her, because if he was there it was because he
knew where the house was. And the fact that he'd gone
away the instant he was recognized, seeing her draw back,
cover her mouth, was even worse, the corner was filled
with an emptiness where doubt was of no use at all, where
everything was certainty and threat, the tree all alone, the
wind in its leaves.

She saw him again at sundown, Carlitos was playing
with his electric train and Flora was humming *bagualas* on
the ground floor, the house, inhabited once more, seemed
to be protecting her, helping her doubt, tell herself that
Milo was taller and more robust, that maybe the siesta-
time drowsiness, the blinding light . . . Every so often she
would leave the television set and from as far away as possible look out a window, never the same one but always on
the upper floor because at street level she would have been
more afraid. When she saw him again he was in almost

the same place but on the other side of the tree trunk.
Night was coming on and his silhouette stood out against
the other people passing by, talking and laughing; Villa
del Parque coming out of its lethargy and going to cafés
and movies, the neighborhood night slowly beginning. It
was he, there was no denying it, that unchanged body,
the gesture of the hand lifting the cigarette to his mouth,
the edges of the white bandana, it was Milo, whom she'd
killed five years before after escaping from Mexico, Milo,
whom she'd killed with papers put together with bribes
and accomplices in a studio in Lomas de Zamora where
she had a childhood friend left who would do anything for
money and maybe for friendship too, Milo, whom she'd
killed with a heart attack in Mexico for Germán, because
Germán wasn't a man to accept anything else, Germán
and his career, his colleagues and his club and his parents,
Germán to get married and set up a family, the chalet and
Carlitos and Flora and the car and the country place in
Manzanares, Germán and so much money, security, then
deciding, almost without thinking about it, sick of misery
and waiting, after the second meeting with Germán at
the Recanatis', the trip to Lomas de Zamora to entrust
herself to the one who had said no at first, that it was an
outrage, that it couldn't be done, that it would take a lot
of pesos, that all right, that in two weeks, that agreed,
Emilio Díaz dead in Mexico of a heart attack, almost the
truth because she and Milo had lived like dead people
during those last months in Coyoacán, until the plane
that brought her back to what was hers in Buenos Aires,
to everything that had belonged to Milo before going to
Mexico together and falling apart together in a war of

silences and deceptions and stupid reconciliations that
weren't worth anything, the curtain ready for the new act,
for a new night of long knives.

The cigarette was still burning slowly in Milo's mouth
as he leaned against the tree, looking unhurriedly at the
windows of the house. How could he have found out?
Matilde thought, still clinging to that absurdity of thinking something was there, but outside or ahead of any
thought. Of course he'd ended up finding out about it,
discovering in Buenos Aires that he was dead because in
Buenos Aires he was dead in Mexico, finding out had
probably humiliated him and lashed him down to the first
gust of rage that whipped his face, pulling him into a
return flight, guiding him through a maze of foreseeable
inquiries, maybe Cholo or Marina, maybe the Recanatis' mother, the old hangouts, the cafés where the gang
gathered, the hunches, and thereabouts the definite news,
that she'd married Germán Morales, man, but just tell me
how can that be, I tell you she got married in church and
everything, the Moraleses, you know, textiles and dough,
respectability, old man, respectability, but just tell me
how can that be since she said, but we thought that you,
it can't be, brother. Of course it couldn't be and that's why
it was all the more so, it was Matilde behind the curtain
spying on him, time immobilized in a present that contained everything, Mexico and Buenos Aires and the heat
of siesta time and the cigarette that kept going up to his
mouth, at some moment nothingness again, the empty
corner, Flora calling her because Carlitos wouldn't take
his bath, the telephone with Perla, restless, not tonight
Perla, it must be my stomach, you go by yourself or with

Negra, it's quite painful, I'd better go to bed, I'll call you tomorrow, and all the time no, it can't be like that, how come they haven't told Germán by now if they knew, he didn't find the house through them, it couldn't have been through them, the Recanatis' mother would have called Germán immediately just for the scene it would cause, to be the first to tell him because she'd never accepted her as Germán's wife, think of the horror, bigamy, I always said she wasn't to be trusted, but nobody had called Germán or maybe they had but at the office and Germán was now far away on a trip, the Recanatis' mother is certainly waiting for him to tell him in person, so she won't lose anything, she or somebody else, Milo had found where Germán lived from somebody, he couldn't have found the chalet by chance, he couldn't be there smoking against the tree by chance. And if he wasn't there now it didn't matter, and double-locking the doors didn't matter, although Flora was a little surprised, the only thing for sure was the bottle of sleeping pills, so that after hours and hours she'd stop thinking and lose herself in a drowsiness broken by dreams where Milo never . . . but in the morning now the shriek when she felt a hand, Carlitos, who wanted to surprise her, the sobbing of Carlitos, offended, and Flora taking him out for a walk, lock the door, Flora. Getting up and seeing him again, there, looking directly at the window without the slightest gesture, drawing back and spying later from the kitchen and nothing, beginning to realize that she was locked up in the house and that it couldn't go on like that, that sooner or later she'd have to go out to take Carlitos to the pediatrician or get together with Perla who was phoning every day and getting impa-

tient and didn't understand. In the orange and asphyxiat-
ing afternoon, Milo leaning against the tree, the black
windbreaker in all that heat, the smoke rising up and
floating away. Or just the tree, but Milo all the same,
Milo all the same, being erased only a little by the pills
and the television until the last program.

On the third day Perla arrived unannounced, tea and
scones and Carlitos, Flora taking advantage of a moment
alone to tell Perla that it couldn't go on like that, Miss
Matilde needs distraction, she spends her days locked up,
I don't understand, Miss Perla, I'm telling you even if it's
not my place to, and Perla smiling at her in the study, you
did the right thing, child, I know that you love Matilde
and Carlitos very much, I think it's Germán's being away
that's depressing her, and Flora without a word lowering
her head, the mistress needs distraction, I'm only telling
you even if it's not my place to. Tea and the usual gossip, nothing about Perla that made her suspect, but then
how had Milo been able, impossible to imagine that the
Recanatis' mother would have been silent so long if she
knew, not even for the pleasure of waiting for Germán and
telling him for the sake of the Lord Jesus or something
like that, she tricked you so you'd lead her down the aisle,
that's exactly what that old witch would say and Germán
falling down out of the clouds, it can't be, it can't be. But,
yes, it could be, except that now she didn't even have the
confirmation that she hadn't been dreaming, that all she
had to do was go to the window, but not with Perla there,
another cup of tea, tomorrow we'll go to the movies, I
promise, come pick me up in your car, I don't know what's
got into me these days, come in your car and we'll go to

the movies, the window there beside the easy chair, but not with Perla there, waiting for Perla to leave and then Milo on the corner, peaceful against the wall as if waiting for a bus, the black windbreaker and the bandana around his neck and then nothing until Milo again.

On the fifth day she saw him follow Flora, who was going to the store, and everything became future, something like the pages remaining in that novel left face down on a sofa, something already written and which it wasn't even necessary to read because it had already happened before being read, had already happened before happening in the reading. She saw them coming back chatting, Flora timid and somewhat mistrustful, saying good-bye on the corner and crossing rapidly. Perla came in her car to pick her up, Milo wasn't there and he wasn't there when they got back late at night either, but in the morning she saw him waiting for Flora, who was going to the market, now he went directly over to her and Flora shook hands with him, they laughed and he took the basket and afterward carried it back filled with the fruit and vegetables, accompanied her to the door, Matilde no longer saw them because the balcony jutted out over the sidewalk, but Flora was taking a long time to come in, they were standing there a while chatting by the door. The next day Flora took Carlitos shopping with her and she saw the three of them laughing and Milo stroked Carlitos on the head, on his return Carlitos was carrying a plush lion and said that Flora's boyfriend had given it to him. So you have a boyfriend, Flora, the two of them alone in the living room. I don't know, ma'am, he's so nice, we met all of a sudden, he went shopping with

me, he's so good with Carlitos, you don't really mind, do
you, ma'am? Telling her no, that was her business, but she
should be careful, a young girl like her, and Flora lowering her eyes and of course, ma'am, he just goes with me
and we talk, he owns a restaurant in Almagro, his name
is Simón. And Carlitos with a magazine in colors, Simón
bought it for me, Mama, that's Flora's boyfriend.

    Germán telephoned from Salta announcing that he'd
be back in about ten days, love, everything fine. The
dictionary said: bigamy, marriage contracted after wid-
owhood by the surviving spouse. It said: status of a man
married to two women or of a woman married to two
men. It said: interpretative bigamy, according to canon
law, that acquired by a marriage contracted with a woman
who has lost her virginity through having prostituted
herself or through having declared her first marriage null
and void. It said: bigamist, one who marries for a second
time without the death of the first spouse. She'd opened
the dictionary without knowing why, as if that could
change anything, she knew it was impossible to change
anything, impossible to go out onto the street and talk to
Milo, impossible to appear at the window and summon
him with a gesture, impossible to tell Flora that Simón
wasn't Simón, impossible to take the plush lion and the
magazine away from Carlitos, impossible to confide in
Perla, just being there, seeing him, knowing that the novel
thrown onto the sofa was written down to the words The
End, that she couldn't change anything, whether she read
it or not, even if she burned it or hid it in the back of Germán's library. Ten days and then yes, but what, Germán
returning to office and friends, the Recanatis' mother or

Cholo, any one of Milo's friends who'd given him the address of the house, I've got to talk to you Germán, it's something very serious, old man, things would be happening one after the other, first Flora with her cheeks flushed, would you mind, ma'am, if Simón came to have coffee in the kitchen with me, just for a little while? Of course she wouldn't mind, how could she mind since it was broad daylight and just for a little while, Flora had every right to receive him in the kitchen and give him a cup of coffee, and Carlitos had every right to come down and play with Simón, who'd brought him a wind-up duck that walked and everything. Staying upstairs until she heard the knock on the door, Carlitos coming up with the duck and Simón told me he's for the River team, that's too bad, Mama, I'm for San Lorenzo, look what he gave me, look how it walks, but look, Mama, it looks like a real duck, Simón gave it to me, he's Flora's boyfriend, why didn't you come down to meet him?

Now she could look out the windows without the slow useless precautions, Milo no longer standing by the tree, every afternoon he would come at five and spend half an hour in the kitchen with Flora and almost always with Carlitos, sometime Carlitos would come up before he left and Matilde knew why, knew that in these few minutes when they were alone what had to happen was being prepared, what was already there as in the novel open on the sofa was being prepared in the kitchen, in the house of somebody who could be anybody at all, the Recanatis' mother or Cholo, a week had passed and Germán telephoned from Córdoba to confirm his return, announcing almond paste for Carlitos and a surprise for Matilde, he would stay home and rest up for five days, they would go out, go to restaurants, go horseback riding at the Manzanares place. That night she telephoned Perla just to hear her talk, hanging on to her voice for an hour until she couldn't anymore because Perla was beginning to realize that all that was artificial, that something was going on with Matilde, you should go see Graciela's analyst, you're acting strange, Matilde, believe me. When she hung up she couldn't even go to the window, she knew that it was already useless that night, that she wouldn't see Milo on the corner which was dark now. She went down to be with Carlitos while Flora served him his dinner, she listened to him complain about the soup even though Flora looked at her, expecting her to intervene, to help her before she put him to bed, while Carlitos resisted and insisted on staying up in the living room playing with the duck and watching television. The whole ground floor was like a different zone; she'd never understood too well why Germán had insisted on putting Carlitos's bedroom next door to the living room, so far from them upstairs, but Germán couldn't stand any noise in the morning, so Flora could get Carlitos ready for school and Carlitos could shout and sing, she kissed him by the bedroom door and went back to the kitchen, although she no longer had anything to do there, looked at the door to Flora's room, went over and touched the knob, opened it a little and saw Flora's bed, the bureau with photographs of rock bands and the singer Mercedes Sosa, she thought she heard Flora coming out of Carlitos's bedroom and she closed it quietly and started to look in the refrigerator. I made mushrooms the way you like them, Miss Matilde, I'll bring up your dinner in half an hour since you're not going out; I've also got a pumpkin dessert that turned out very good, just like in my village, Miss Matilde.

The stairway was poorly lighted but the steps were few and wide, she went up almost without looking, the bedroom door ajar with a beam of light breaking on the waxed landing. She'd been eating at the little table beside the window for several days now, the dining room downstairs was so solemn without Germán, everything fit on a tray and Flora, agile, almost enjoying the fact that Miss Matilde was eating upstairs now that the master was away, stayed with her and they talked for a while and Matilde would have liked Flora to have eaten with her, but Carlitos would have told Germán and Germán the discourse on distance and respect, Flora herself would have been afraid because Carlitos always ended up finding out everything and would have told Germán. And now what could she talk about to Flora when the only thing possible was to get the bottle she'd hidden behind the books and drink half a glass of whiskey in one swig, choke and pant and pour herself another drink, almost beside the window opening onto the night, onto the nothingness there outside where nothing was going to happen, not even the repetition of the shadow beside the tree, the glow of the cigarette going up and down like an indecipherable signal, perfectly clear.

She threw the mushrooms out the window while Flora prepared the tray with the dessert, she heard her coming up with that rhythm like a sleigh or a runaway colt that Flora had when she came up the stairs, told her that the mushrooms were delicious, praised the color of the pump-

kin dessert, asked for a double cup of strong coffee, and
for her to bring her up another pack of cigarettes from the
living room. It's hot tonight, Miss Matilde, we'll have to
leave the windows open wide, I'll spray some insecticide
before we go to bed, I've already put Carlitos in, he went
right to sleep and you saw how he was complaining, he
misses his daddy, poor thing, and then Simón was telling
him stories this afternoon. Tell me if you need anything,
Miss Matilde, I'd like to go to bed early if you don't mind.
Of course she didn't mind even though Flora had never
said anything like that before, she would finish her work
and shut herself up in her room to listen to the radio or
knit, she looked at her for a moment and Flora smiled at
her, content, she was carrying the tray with the coffee and
she went down to get the insecticide, I'd best leave it here
on the dresser, Miss Matilde, you can spray it yourself
before you go to bed, because no matter what they say, it
does have a bad smell, it's best when you're getting ready
to go to bed. She closed the door, the colt tripped lightly
down the stairs, one last sound of dishes; the night began
in exactly that second when Matilde went into the library
to get the bottle and bring it over beside the easy chair.

The low light from the lamp barely reached the bed at
the back of the room, vaguely visible were one of the night
tables and the sofa where the novel had been left, but it
wasn't there anymore, after so many days Flora must have
decided to put it on the empty shelf in the library. With
the second whiskey Matilde heard ten o'clock strike in
some distant belfry, she thought that she'd never heard
that bell before, counted each ring and looked at the
telephone, maybe Perla, but no, not Perla at that hour,

she always got annoyed or she wasn't in. Or Alcira, calling Alcira and telling her, just telling her that she was
afraid, that it was stupid but maybe if Mario hadn't gone
out with the car, something like that. She didn't hear the
street door open but it didn't matter, it was absolutely clear
that the main door was being opened or was going to be
opened and nothing could be done, she couldn't go out to
the landing, lighting it with the lamp from the bedroom
and looking down into the living room, she couldn't ring
the bell for Flora to come, the insecticide was there, the
water too for medicine and thirst, the turned-down bed
waiting. She went to the window and saw the empty
corner; maybe if she'd looked out before she would have
seen Milo approaching, crossing the street, and disappearing under the balcony, but it would have been even
worse, what could she have shouted to Milo, how could
she have stopped him since he was going to come into
the house, since Flora was going to open the door and
receive him in her room, Flora even worse than Milo at
that moment, Flora who would have learned everything,
who would have her revenge on Milo by having revenge
on her, dragging her down into the mud, on Germán,
involving her in a scandal. There wasn't the slightest possibility for anything left, but neither could it have been
she who'd cried out the truth, completely impossible was
an absurd hope that Milo was only coming for Flora,
that some incredible turn of fate had shown him Flora
completely separate from the other business, that the
corner there had been just any corner for Milo back in
Buenos Aires, that Milo didn't know it was Germán's
house, didn't know he was dead back there in Mexico,

that Milo wasn't looking for her through Flora's body. Staggering drunkenly over to the bed, she pulled off the clothing that clung to her body; naked, she rolled onto her side on the bed and looked for the bottle of pills, the final pink or green port within reach of her hand. It was hard to get the pills out and Matilde piled them up on the night table without looking at them, her eyes lost on the shelves where the novel was, she could see it very clearly, open and face down on the one empty shelf where Flora had put it, she saw the Malayan knife that Cholo had given Germán, the crystal ball on the base of red velvet. She was sure that the door had opened downstairs, that Milo had come into the house, into Flora's room, was probably talking to Flora or had already begun to undress her, because for Flora that had to be the only reason Milo was there, gaining access to her room in order to undress her and undress himself, kissing her, let me, let me stroke you like this, and Flora resisting and not today, Simón, I'm afraid, let me, but Simón in no hurry, little by little he'd laid her crosswise on the bed and was kissing her hair, looking for her breasts under her blouse, resting a leg on her thighs and taking off her shoes as if playing, talking into her ear and kissing her closer and closer to her mouth, I want you, my love, let me undress you, let me see you, you're so beautiful, moving away the lamp and enwrapping her in shadows and caresses, Flora giving in with a first whimper, the fear that something will be heard upstairs, that Miss Matilde or Carlitos, but no, speak low, leave me like this now, the clothes falling just anywhere, the tongues finding each other, the moans, Simón, please don't hurt me, it's the first time, Simón, I know, stay just like that, be quiet now, don't cry out, love, don't cry out.

She cried out but into Simón's mouth as he knew the moment, holding her tongue between his teeth and sinking his fingers into her hair, she cried out and then she wept under Simón's hands as he covered her face, caressing it, she went limp with a final Mama, Mama, a whimper that passed into a panting and a sweet and soft sob, a my love, love, the bland season of blended bodies, of the hot breath of night. Much later, after two cigarettes against a backrest of pillows, towels between guilt-ridden thighs, the words, the plans that Flora babbled out as in a dream, the hope that Simón was listening, smiling at her, kissing her breasts, moving a slow spider of fingers across her stomach, letting himself go, drowsing, doze off a bit, I'm going to the bathroom and I'll be right back, I don't need any light, I'm like a night cat, I know where it is, and Flora no, they might hear you, Simón don't be silly, I told you I'm like a cat and I know where the door is, doze off a bit, I'll be right back, that's it, nice and quiet.

He closed the door as if to add a bit more silence to the house, naked, he crossed the kitchen and the dining room, faced the stairs and put his foot on the first step, feeling around for it. Good wood, a good house Germán Morales has. On the third step he saw the mark of the beam of light from under the bedroom door; he went up the other four steps and put his hand on the knob, opened the door with one push. The blow against the dresser reached Carlitos in his restless sleep, he sat up in bed and cried out, he cried out a lot at night and Flora would get up to calm him, give him some water before

Germán could get angry. She knew she had to quiet Carlitos because Simón hadn't come back yet, she had to calm him down before Miss Matilde got worried, she wrapped herself in the sheet and ran to Carlitos's room, found him sitting at the foot of the bed staring into space, shouting with fear, she picked him up in her arms, talking to him, telling him no, no, she was there, she'd bring him some chocolate, she'd leave the light on, she heard the incomprehensible cry and went into the living room with Carlitos in her arms, the stairway was illumined by the light from above, she reached the foot of the stairs and saw them in the doorway, staggering, the naked bodies wrapped in a single mass that fell slowly onto the landing, that slipped down the steps, that without breaking apart rolled downstairs in a confused tangle until it stopped motionless on the living room rug, the knife planted in Simón's chest as he spread out on his back, and Matilde—but that only the autopsy would show afterward—that she had taken enough sleeping pills to kill her two hours later, when I arrived with the ambulance and was giving Flora an injection to bring her out of her hysteria, giving Carlitos a sedative, and asking the nurse to stay until relatives or friends got there.

Translated by Gregory Rabassa

The Man with Blue Eyes

Alicia Steimberg

I SAW HIM BEFORE HE SAW ME. He looked his age, sixty, as he would later tell me. He wore an overcoat and scarf, quite sensibly, because a deceptive, icy wind was blowing down Avenida San Juan, the kind that fosters your hopes of a real winter in Buenos Aires. In his right hand he carried a briefcase. He was slightly stooped, just slightly: it would be more accurate to say that his posture

---

ALICIA STEIMBERG (1933–) Born in Buenos Aires, Steimberg is the descendant of Ukrainian-Romanian immigrants who were among the early settlers of the Entre Rios Jewish colonies. Her writing has earned her numerous accolades including the prestigious *Premio Planeta* award for her novel *Cuando digo Magdalena* (*Call Me Magdalena*, 1992) and a Fulbright Fellowship in support of her participation in the 1983 Iowa International Writers' Conference. Steimberg is also an experienced teacher, as illustrated by the story at hand from her collection *Aprender a escribir: fatigas y delicias de una escritora y sus alumnos* (*Learn How to Write: Trials and Delights of a Writer and Her Students*, 2006).

---

wasn't perfectly erect. He was staring into the window in
the door of the building, through which he hoped to see
me appear, but I, too, was in the street, getting out of a
taxi, and I had time for a quick glimpse of my watch. It
was five minutes to seven, the hour we had agreed on for
his interview before he started his classes with me. When
I approached him from behind, he turned around immediately, and I saw what he always tried to flaunt: his blue
eyes and his white, even teeth. But, what of it? A person
doesn't allow herself to be conquered by a pair of eyes or a
set of teeth, but rather by a man's gaze and his smile. And
this man didn't have either. At that moment he had only
eyes and teeth.

"I came early," he said, by way of apology. "That's a
kind of breach of punctuality in itself," he added, smiling more broadly. We were already in the elevator, on our
way upstairs. He had gray hair, in tight waves. When we
reached my floor, he stepped aside to let me out first, and
as I headed toward the end of the corridor, I felt a scream
coming on. But I reached my apartment without incident,
and only after we were inside, with the door closed and
locked behind us, did I regret having agreed to the interview. There he was, sitting stiffly before me with his overcoat and scarf draped over the back of a chair, his briefcase
on the table, and his polite, silent gaze fixed on me, which
prompted me to spring from my chair and head straight
to the kitchen to offer him tea, coffee, water, because he
immediately replied all right, some coffee, thank you.

Alone in the kitchen, as I put the kettle on to boil and
placed the cups on a tray, I started to feel more relaxed.
After all, I've been receiving strangers in my home for

years, people I've only spoken with on the telephone. I don't give out certain information by email; I insist on a phone call before deciding whether I'd welcome a weekly visit to my house from someone who expresses himself in that particular way. At the end of the interview, some of them tell me frankly they won't be coming; they had expected something different. Who knows what they were expecting? I advertise classes in learning to write more freely, and they seek me out enthusiastically, telling me yes, precisely, their writing is locked up, and they want to set it free. But by the end of the interview, many of them remember that they have to take a trip first; maybe when they get back . . .

I've never seen any of those mysterious travelers again. But this gentleman, Félix Antonucci was his name, said he would come, and he did, not even missing class the day his mother was buried. In effect, his mother died barely two weeks after he started classes, and yet he showed up, not the very day she died, possibly because it wasn't his regular day, but the next, two hours after the funeral. With great fortitude he said that what had happened to his mother was very sad, but instead of mourning her, he preferred to remember her as alive and young.

I read the text he took from his briefcase, mentally trying to supply those things the author didn't say, as one does when reading. If a text mentions a skinny man with bags under his eyes, the reader quickly imagines a skinny man with bags under his eyes, but there are as many skinny, baggy-eyed men as there are readers. Félix Antonucci said that he had spent his childhood and adolescence in a "sausage house" in the lower Flores District, the kind

with lots of rooms in a row, all facing a patio. So had
I. I imagined the entryway of my house, separated from
the patio by a wall of colored panes of glass in a metallic
frame. But I couldn't keep imagining; I had to continue
reading, under the attentive gaze of my pupil. Now he *did*
have a gaze, but it wasn't a seductive one. Rather, it was
one that wanted to know. It wanted to know my opinion.

The text said nothing more about the house, but instead
talked about four characters that were having lunch: an
eight-year-old boy, his mother and father, and a friend
of the father's, a recent widower. Maybe that was why,
Antonucci said, interrupting my reading, the friend was
such a frequent lunch guest at that house. And he started
to say something else about him, but I don't remember
what because I had stopped listening. I struggled to visualize the interior of the Antonuccis' house, beyond the
entry hall, but I could think only of my old childhood
home. I didn't want to picture them in the dining room
of that house, either, because it's a sanctuary that can be
trespassed by strangers only in dreams.

Nevertheless, after returning to the reading, I managed to visualize the dining room, and in a piece of
dining room furniture, a drawer with green felt-lined
compartments containing knives, forks, soup spoons, and
teaspoons, the spoons eternally jumbled together with
baby utensils, untouched since the beginning of my life,
and a single, squat ice cream spoon that came from God
knows where. In the front compartment, horizontal and
wider than the rest, were the ladle, the carving knife, and
the serving pieces. And four pairs of my mother's knit-
ting needles, of various widths. In my mind, I packed

Antonucci's diners into the entry hall, near the front door, and it didn't matter one bit because immediately they left off eating lunch in order to chase after the boy, who had escaped through that door.

The next few classes, with Antonucci in full mourning and his writing evoking his early days as an only child, gave no indication of the direction he was about to take.

"No, I've never been to a literary workshop or tried to write anything on my own," he replied to my question, unsurprisingly.

I dedicated a few moments to observing how meticulously he had dressed and groomed himself for the occasion. I imagined him inspecting himself in the mirror, in full face and in profile, before going out the door. He wore a hand-knitted, bluish green sweater of very fine quality, and he looked at me with those little blue eggs set in the visible part of the white spheres of his eyes. He bowed his head slightly, as men do when they want to appear more intense.

"Yes, I've read Borges, Sabato, Bioy Casares, Arlt. So what?"

His expression was that of someone who didn't give a damn about anything at all. His two hands pressed flat on the table, a wedding ring on the left one, his manicured nails, his protruding lower lip, made me think of a compulsive gambler who has nevertheless taken pains with his appearance so as not to lose absolutely everything. I changed the subject. Earlier in the week I had received an email from him containing a text about a sharpshooter who never succeeded in killing anyone.

"Interesting," I remarked, "a sharpshooter with bad aim."

He closed his mouth, straightened up, and flashed me one of those blue-eyed glances you see in 1950s North American films. I heard the kettle whistling. I dashed to the kitchen and from there called him in to chat with me, as other pupils do, while I made tea.

"Thank you for your confidence," he said. I pointed him toward a chair next to the little table. As he sat down he asked, "May I?"

All the while he said thank you, may I, and please; he always stepped aside to let me leave the elevator first; and after taking off his overcoat he would wait, standing beside his chair, until I sat down. He always signed his email messages "Very truly yours," followed by his name. And yet the language he used in his writing went beyond the colloquial: it bordered on profanity and would have been difficult for a young reader to understand. But I believed him when he told me that the expression "You have the nuts to ride a bike by yourself" was common when he was a boy.

"What's this?" I asked, on seeing the expression in a story of his childhood that attempted to depict his mother as young and vital. "I've never heard this."

"You never heard what?"

"I never heard anyone say, '*You have the nuts.*' What does it mean?"

"Oh. It means 'You're brave; you have the nerve to ride a bike by yourself.'"

"Ah," I replied, and I confess it actually struck me

funny. "Well, I've never head that before," I remarked. "In any case no one says it anymore."

The equivalent expression these days, I thought, would be, "So you have the balls to . . ." *et cetera,* but I said nothing. I didn't like the turn this conversation was taking.

"Look, Félix, in any case it must have been a very local expression. But if people read it in Venezuela, or in Ecuador . . ."

It wasn't the first time I had tried to convince a student of the convenience of using more or less universal language, because a writer has to understand that his book will be read in all the Spanish-speaking countries, with their differences in vocabulary, and it's best to avoid the need for footnotes or for obliging the reader to flip awkwardly to the last pages of the book in order to consult a glossary.

I paused because I saw that the man, so polite and correct on other occasions, was paying me not the slightest attention, but was instead intently devouring one biscuit after another from the batch on the tea tray. When I stopped speaking, he said:

"Go on, finish reading the story."

"Look, Antonucci," I replied, pushing the pages away, "I've already told you that if there's a problem in the text, you have to analyze it and resolve it before you move on."

"Yes, I know. But keep reading, so you'll have a better sense of the whole thing."

I'll spare the reader the tedious discussion that followed concerning what mattered more, the details or the whole, and Antonucci's desire to use exactly the same expression his father had used, an expression that was very familiar to him. Suddenly it all struck me as pointless, because the text was greatly flawed, and one expression was just as good as another. In any event, no one capable of evaluating a text would ever accept this one for publication.

For the last portion of the class, I proposed reading the beginning of Borges's "The Aleph." Even those who have already read it can't help admiring the way in which the character Borges alludes to the death, or rather to the definitive absence, of Beatriz Viterbo by mentioning some billboards in Plaza Constitución with an ad for a brand of cigarette. He doesn't say that Beatriz Viterbo would never again see the successive changes, but rather that the billboards, the new one and those yet to come, *were already slipping away from her,* together with the other infinite changes in the universe that she would never see, either. Antonucci seemed to relax somewhat during this reading, and the class concluded with the usual protocol.

It was too early in his training process to ask him to revise the text. I've discovered that if I insist on revision before my pupils have figured out for themselves how hard it is to write, they tend to follow the same mysterious path of those who take off on a trip after their initial interview. Besides, the little story had its good points: for example, the character of the mother as a model housewife who assumes full control of her chores, like a doctor who won't allow his patient to choose a medication by himself. Even for a simple matter like mopping up a drop of water that had spilled on the oilcloth table cover, she would hurry to the kitchen, her face contorted by her sense of fulfilling a duty, not allowing herself even a trace of a smile as she dried the spill or returned to the kitchen with the rag. The father was a more flexible person who tried not to upset his wife, but Antonucci told me he couldn't be sure his father had always been faithful to her. I responded that what he had just revealed verbally should appear in the text, or else it would be of no value: his readers had no way of guessing. At that moment he seemed very enthusiastic, reacting only with an affirmative nod as he crammed the biscuits into his mouth. We looked like two architects in a pre-computer age, sketching on a drawing board to the strains of a radio tune at four in the morning: exhausted and ignoring one another.

That week I received his text by email and decided to declare it completed. At my suggestion, the author had added a paragraph about the kind of punishment his mother administered when he didn't obey her orders to come in from playing in the street: she beat him. If he did come home on time, but had muddied his new shoes, she beat him anyway. Félix Antonucci didn't complain about the beatings: I guess he thought they were a sound method of instruction.

I told him to submit the text (he called it a story) to one of the two thousand short story contests held every year in Spain. This time, before he left, he confided that he was already thinking about another story.

I planned my classes carefully, taking pains to keep them from seeming boring. Those were the coldest days that winter, which, as always in Buenos Aires, wasn't especially harsh. Antonucci showed up several times in the same bluish green sweater, which accentuated the color of his eyes. It suited him quite well, unlike the overcoat, which aged him because it was gray, a very classic style, and because it was an overcoat. It called attention to the fact that he was an older person trying to avoid pneumonia. But once he had taken it off, settled into his seat, and absorbed the warmth of the atmosphere and the fragrance of the tea and biscuits, he was almost pleasant.

He opened his briefcase, pulled out some papers, and handed them to me.

I can hardly speak of the opening of the new text, because one characteristic of, let's say, inexperienced authors, is that they are unable to take their time, stop and glance around, delay revelations. Instead, they charge headlong: everything is made known immediately, but nothing is really known, because the characters aren't fleshed out. Even if they've killed someone, the reader wouldn't think of throwing them in jail, because it would be like incarcerating a crayon stick figure drawn by a five-year-old. The opposite happens when they write dialogue, long conversations filled with useless details and clichés, in which a character tries to convince another of something. This one was a dialogue between a store manager and a vagrant who meet out in the country when the store manager gets a flat tire and the vagrant helps him change it.

I spoke to Antonucci about the need to achieve a denser, more detailed style, but he replied that even before beginning to write the text, he already knew what he wanted to achieve: to show the reader that a store manager and a tramp were identical pieces of shit. I told him that readers of short stories and novels aren't too interested in being convinced of anything; they're simply people who like to look at the lives of others through a peephole, and it's necessary to satisfy their curiosity.

"But these characters just want to talk," Antonucci said.

"Fine," I agreed, "but it's impossible for two people to sustain a very long conversation without one of them going off to close a window or make some coffee, or just go to the bathroom."

I gave him ten minutes to reread the text and make a few changes while I headed for the kitchen to make more tea. When I returned, the page Antonucci had been working on was lying on my place setting, and he was looking out the window.

In the revised paragraph one of the characters remarked:

"Just a minute, please. I have to pee."

My jaw clenched. Was Antonucci serious, or was he making fun of me?

"Don't you like it?" he asked. "I knew it would irritate you."

"Yes, it irritates me," I replied.

"You said women don't talk like that," Antonucci recalled. "But these are two men. And my wife, who's a professor of economics, assures me that she says *pee*."

Antonucci hadn't written that text for today's class, but rather before he met me. I decided to do a superficial evaluation without dwelling on my irritation. My conversation with him had been reduced to a discussion of which words men use and which words women use.

Finally he brought in another text in which the main character was a girl from the provinces (without even mentioning which province) who finds a job as a waitress. Antonucci's text used that term, "waitress," a word that might have been popular some years ago—and was, indeed, the term I favored as a youngster when I discovered that women could be admitted to that profession—but one that had been replaced fairly universally by the generic "waiter" or "server." Suddenly, I don't know how, this young woman begins to speak of her loneliness. Of course, of course, Antonucci explains, when I look at him, a little perplexed, the girl is alone; she has no one here in Buenos Aires; it's natural for her to feel lonely. Yes, yes, I say, and go on reading. The text reads:

"I'm so sad. How lonely I am! I like that dark-haired waiter with green eyes, but I don't trust him. I think he's the type of guy who only wants to pop my cherry."

Astonished, I put the story down, but I was very careful not to say anything to Antonucci until I felt sure that was what he meant. And finally I told him that he was using an inadequate form of language, that the way men talk among themselves is one thing (and I knew whereof I spoke, having taught at a boys' high school where the students didn't care that I was eavesdropping on them), but the way women talked was quite another. Antonucci laughed, saying that his daughters talked that way. "They say *cherry*, they say *cunt*, and my wife, who's a professor of economics, assures me that she says *pee*."

For a moment, the two of us remained silent and motionless, which gave me time to think that *cherry* wasn't just an awful word choice, but that the notion of the intact hymen had gone out of fashion many years ago and didn't concern men very much anymore. In the

ensuing argument (which I was unable to avoid), I said as
much. Antonucci came unhinged: his face grew hard and
he practically spat the words at me: yes, it *did* matter; men
today still cared a great deal about virginity.

The girl from the provinces goes to a dance where she
sees the co-worker she likes so much; they dance, and
he asks her out. After that you can't exactly say that the
events unfold quickly—it's more like one of those ava-
lanches of rocks and earth that hurtle down a mountain-
side, burying an entire town. Before we get to the next
line, there's the girl, standing outside the door of some
sort of shed on a deserted street. On the opposite sidewalk is a wall that fades into the darkness on either side.
Just as the young woman is wondering if she's done the
right thing by agreeing to a rendezvous in such a desolate
spot, the door swings open, someone grabs her brutally
by the arm and drags her inside. The door closes, there's a
bloodcurdling scream, the end.

I smiled so that my student wouldn't notice my dis-
comfort, but I was ready to vomit the biscuit I had just
eaten. I was frightened, not by what I'd read, but by Félix
Antonucci. The class ended fifteen minutes later, following a reading of *The Crocodile* by Felisberto Hernández.
We stopped at the point where the protagonist speaks
of his plans to give piano recitals and sell stockings. As
before, Antonucci calmed down while reading.

Two days later I received an email with the "story" of
the girl from the provinces, the girl who felt so lonely.
When we read it in class, the text was virtually complete,
with an ambiguous, but apparently tragic, ending. As
though it were necessary, Antonucci explained that no

one knew what had happened to the girl. Why had he sent me that text again? Because, following my instructions, he had reread it and thought it a good idea to insert a short paragraph of two or three lines.

"I really like that waiter," the girl said, "but I know what kind of man he is. The only thing he wants is my cunt."

It's incredible that a mature woman like me, more than mature, could have been so offended by that word as to think of putting an immediate end to Antonucci's classes. A word that in nearly all Spanish-speaking countries, some more than others, is associated with the innocent *concha*, conch, "a bivalved mollusk," whose shells can be found anytime at the beach, almost always broken and empty. But we Argentine women, when referring to those bivalves, always say *conchilla*, even though we know that in Spain Concha or Conchita is a common nickname for Concepción, and that there even exists the respectable surname "de la Concha," which is listed in that country's telephone directories. There could well be reputable gentlemen named, for instance, Francisco de la Concha, or José de la Concha. If they do exist, I offer them my respects and beg their pardon for using their most estimable name in this text, and why not recall, while we're at it, *addirittura*, as the Italians would say, an early twentieth-century writer named Concha Espina? I can personally attest to the fact that there was a book by that very writer in my father's house, titled *La esfinge maragata*. Who doesn't know that? I would have cried at age nine or ten if anyone had asked me, who doesn't know that in Papa's library there's a paperback book, with a picture on the cover of a woman with her face hidden behind the black veil of a hat, peering out a train window?

When I discovered Concha Espina's *La esfinge maragata* on the shelves of my parents' library, I was already familiar with the other unthinkable, forbidden, and dark meaning of the word that serves as that writer's first name. I will not allow anyone to laugh or ask me why the meaning is so dark. For fifty or sixty years, the female students at a girls' parochial school in the city of Tucumán, a school whose name I recall perfectly but will refrain from mentioning here out of courtesy and respect for a religion, the Catholic religion, which I always liked and could never belong to because I had been raised by atheist parents and grandparents, who, more than people who didn't believe in God were people who hated a God in whom they certainly believed, because you can't hate a nonexistent being, those students, as I was saying, were not allowed to shower naked; they had to bathe in their nightgowns. If they hadn't possessed a forbidden, dark part of their bodies, why would they have had to keep it eternally covered? I think the poor nuns were surely following the orders of a stern—and equally dark—Mother Superior. May God forgive me for what I'm saying, but . . . isn't forced concealment an incitement to look and discover?

But while the Spanish ocean waves deposit all manner of conch shells—or *conchas*—on the shore, jagged on the outside and slick on the inside, their somber colors muted by time and sea, let us watch as the figure of Félix Antonucci retreats down Calle San Juan beneath a stubborn drizzle, slightly stooped and in his overcoat, after having come to return a book I had lent him. I opened the door, took the book that he held out to me, left the building, and closed the front door, anticipating his desire to enter and confront me in the hallway. I had put on a coat and was carrying my purse, as if at that very moment I too was about to go somewhere. I didn't look him in the eye because I wasn't sure his eyes would still be blue. What if they had turned red? And if he had followed me into the elevator, would he have let me out first, and while I preceded him toward the far end of the corridor, would he have fired a bullet into my back?

After we said goodbye, he turned and began walking away. I crossed the street. From the opposite sidewalk, partially hidden behind a tree, I watched him disappear slowly, perhaps muttering curses at having been suddenly thwarted in his desire to study literature, perhaps shouting at me through clenched teeth, "Stupid bivalved mollusk!" although I don't think that's something a man says to a woman, but rather something a man, or a woman, says to a man.

Translated by Andrea G. Labinger

The Last Happy Family

Marcelo Birmajer

MR. CARPATO HAS ASSIGNED ME to evict them seeing as two years ago I completed a course in social psychology.

"You understand them, Blot, you go," he told me.

As I head toward the corner of Tucumán and Uriburu, where the property in question is located, I realize that in the three years I've been working with Mr. Carpato I'm still uncertain about the proper pronunciation of his surname. I honestly don't know which syllable is supposed to be stressed. Is it CARpato or CarPAto? I'm convinced—since my intuition never fails me in such matters—that it's not CarpaTO. A silly joke always occurs to me. I imagine that Mr. Carpato has "carpet toe," a strange foot condi-

---

MARCELO BIRMAJER (1966–) Perhaps best known for cowriting the film script with director Daniel Burman of *El abrazo partido* (*The Lost Embrace*, 2004), his work often revolves around Buenos Aires's Jewish neighborhood known as Barrio Once. His humor has often been compared to that of Woody Allen's as his characters display a healthy neurosis towards life, literature, and the pursuit of happiness.

tion, like hammertoe, except the toes become infested with a shaggy fungus. I'm sure nothing could be further from the truth, but the joke always crosses my mind.

My job at Carpato's firm does not include evicting people from their home. On the contrary; it's the exact opposite. I'm a real estate agent at Carpato Properties. Mr. Carpato buys and sells properties. I'm one of his sales agents. Therefore, I don't evict people, rather I try to convince them to buy and occupy buildings, apartments, or office space previously purchased by Carpato Properties.

Mr. Carpato has not only bought and sold hundreds of properties, he has also branched out into other business dealings, the details of which I know nothing about. I only know that they include the sale of cheap pizza and hot dogs as well as a parking lot. In the area of real estate—my only concern in the vastness of Carpato's empire—it so happens that there is a homeless family occupying an unfinished building purchased by Carpato, which Pomesano, one of my colleagues, was unable to sell. The property was Pomesano's responsibility, so I wonder why Mr. Carpato is sending me to evict these poor people and not Pomesano.

"You understand them, Blot, you go."

Does he really believe that I'm better prepared thanks to my course in social psychology? Or, on the contrary, does he hate the fact that I took the course, like he hates Bach Flower remedies and yoga classes?

I'll never forget the warning from his blonde, forty-something, robust secretary, Marga, the day of my second interview prior to getting the job. While sitting in the waiting room I pulled out my bottle of Bach Flower drops and was about to give myself a dose when she said to me in a low, dry voice that seemed more like a shout:

"The boss hates Bach Flower remedies." I let the liquid drip to the floor and stuck the dropper in my left pocket (the open bottle spilling into my right one), and since then I haven't taken them again.

I'm all out of questions and memories and I've just about arrived at the building. Would Bach Flower remedies come in handy for throwing a family out of a house that doesn't belong to them? Would they help one to gain the superhuman strength needed to win a fight with the no doubt strapping head of the household? Would they aid in alleviating the guilt in the unlikely event that we come out the victors and the family is forced out onto the street? No? Then they serve no purpose at all.

This is the Once neighborhood. Once, the number eleven. What's up with the name? Is it in homage to an eleventh commandment that nobody's aware of? The still under-construction but occupied building is on Uriburu, after crossing Tucumán some twenty meters in the direction of Viamonte. On one of the corners there still exists an old run-down string factory; the mere sight of it depresses me. In front of the factory stands a yellow two-story house that takes up the entire corner. On the outer wall is still painted, in faded red and with a disturbing insult written below it, the name of a union leader who, if I'm not mistaken, was murdered in 1974. Kitty-corner from the string factory is the Adán Barbershop. It is, by far, the best in the neighborhood, and in fact it is well known throughout all of Buenos Aires. They don't charge outrageous prices and are a must whenever a wedding or bar mitzvah arises. I grew up in this neighborhood, but I only got my hair cut one time at Adán's: the morning of a wedding that ultimately didn't take place. I never went for a haircut there again.

Half a block from there and facing the aforementioned corner, along Uriburu, rises the building that I'm standing in front of now. There's really no entrance to it, no door or gate. Much to my horror, I notice that what was a door two days ago is now little more than a narrow opening in a dirty bricked-up entryway through which the average person would have a heck of a time squeezing his body, let alone a fat man or a pregnant woman.

The family, whose identity remains a mystery, has been squatting on the property for a week and a half. It's a four-story unfinished building that needs balconies, needs paint, needs to be finished. Nevertheless, the invading family is proof enough that it's ready to inhabit. It's not at all unlikely that a piece of the building comes crashing down on them at any moment, but it would seem that such a risk is less of a threat than exposure to the elements.

On Mr. Carpato's orders, we go out and sell buildings or apartments that are near completion, like in this case, but clearly Pomesano will not be able to sell this property nor a single tile in it as long as the trespassers remain there. It's remarkable that in two days they have transformed what was the front door into a brick barrier with a slot-like opening for an entrance. They must be laborers or craftsmen of some sort: bricklayers or potters, cabinetmakers or basket weavers. Well, it doesn't much matter. I shouldn't get distracted from the main objective.

I clap my hands together. There's no doorbell so I clap and call out:

"Is there anyone home?"

I repeat the question a couple of times and clap again. I look like a mental patient applauding his own recital. Finally a feminine voice, somewhat hostile and in an accent I can't recognize, asks:

"What's wrong?"

I don't know how to respond. I opt to speak to her as if she were one of the maids I encounter when I'm out selling properties door to door.

"Is the man of the house here?" I ask.

"What man?" asks the strange, hostile voice.

"The man of the house," I repeat.

"No," says the voice, which I discern is that of an adolescent girl. "The man isn't here," she snickers.

Given the girl's age, I bring myself to reformulate the question.

"Is your papa home?"

"My papa? Yes, he's here. Papa!" She yelps for her father.

Silence ensues. Suddenly the girl lets out a joyful shriek of surprise, and I hear the voice of a man. It's also hostile, succinct and in an accent I don't recognize.

"What do you want?"

"I work for Mr. Carpato," I say. "This property belongs to him."

"Yeah, I know it belongs to me," the man says. He lets out a loud, high-pitched laugh accompanied by that of his daughter and another woman.

"No," I reply. "It belongs to Mr. Carpato. We could

have the police evict you today, but we aren't that insensitive. If you leave by tomorrow morning, we are prepared to give you five-hundred dollars.

The reference to our insensitivity is false. We can't have the police evict them today.

"I don't care about the money," the man says. "I have no use for it. Come back early tomorrow morning."

"You'll leave then?" I ask.

"Come tomorrow morning and we'll discuss it."

"But you must vacate the premises," I insist.

The opening falls silent and now that my sight has adjusted I make out the movement of the man in the dark returning to the damp interior.

I glance at the upper stories of the building and notice white garments hanging from the balconyless window of the second floor. One of them has a red stain on it. Before leaving, I place my eye to the opening but the stench repels me from remaining that close for even a second. I step back and take in a breath of air, managing with effort to fight back the nausea.

I have trouble remembering my brief marriage. I'm reminiscing now as I walk down Tucumán Street toward Callao Avenue and then down Callao to the street named for a pornographic national hero, Pacheco de Melo, where Lucía lives.

I was walking along this street, but on the other side, toward Paso, the day that I was on my way to get married. Lucía was waiting for me at the *shul* on Paso Street.

During the four years that our relationship lasted, my feelings for Lucía remained constant and confusing. Constant, because they never varied. Confusing, because if it

were a matter of feeling merely affection, chastity would
have needed to be involved. Although I don't know what
love is, I'm sure it wasn't whatever we had. In a nutshell
it's hard to say, but while I was sexually satiated by Lucía
I never loved her more than you would love a second
cousin. If I felt really lonely, I felt less alone with her. If
I was upset, her caress would calm me down. Back then
Lucía was a fresh body and a mouth that was a delight to
kiss. At times it seemed strange to me that I didn't love
her more than I did, or do. She's grown older. Besides,
not that I'm trying to justify myself, but her rudeness
would have destroyed even the devotion of someone truly
in love with her. Perhaps the reason why I wasn't able
to intensely love her—I think as bus 124 almost runs me
over one block from Pacheco de Melo—is that we have
two very different personalities. Lucía is a dreamer and
I am more of a realist. I ask myself: Why do I need to
go around looking for reasons to explain my feelings for
Lucía? What do I have to explain? For whatever reason,
the matter makes me nervous and I have the urge to place
a few Bach Flower drops on my tongue. But ever since
Marga yelled at me I haven't been able to touch the bottle.

Beyond the right or wrong of why Lucía is a dreamer,
she just is. It was she who two years ago insisted that I
finish the course in social psychology that she herself
began but never completed. It was she who four years into
our relationship and uninterrupted sexual relations com-
pelled me to say yes to her marriage proposal because our
relationship and relations had matured; she who found
the Reform rabbi; she who waited for me at the entrance
to the synagogue and told me that she couldn't marry

me because there was no passion in our relationship; and it was she who, ultimately, urged me to keep seeing her and to not discontinue the frequency or the nature of our encounters.

Although it seemed that for her nothing had changed, for me things had. For example, I would never accept another marriage proposal from her. I wouldn't say "I do" even if she were to tell me that our relationship had matured again. What's more, I will not have children with her. Before, I wouldn't have minded, but now I am determined not to. No matter how much she pleads, arguing that old age is just around the corner and that her biological clock is winding down. I'm conservative, and if I don't get married, I won't have kids. And I refuse to marry Lucía. In spite of that, the elevator is taking me to her now. She denies me nothing even though I deny her everything. She kisses me and I sense a new wrinkle just above her lip. It fills me with sadness.

To think that it's already been six years since her grandmother introduced us with the hope that we would someday marry. Her grandmother, now there's a woman with whom I could have fallen truly in love.

I don't know whether to tell Lucía about the squatter family before or after we hit the sheets. If I tell her before she'll respond with a lengthy lecture, and the truth is I'm pretty damn horny. If I keep it to myself I'll be antsy in bed. Besides, for some time now after a roll in the hay I don't have the energy to talk to Lucía. Perhaps I'm feeling less comfortable about the nature of our relationship and leaning toward something on a purely sexual level, with no hint of affection or companionship, a change that, paradoxically, would bring us closer to what—I once read—passion really means.

Lucía claims that her round, white bed is her only temple. She makes statements like that all the time. I think it's a lie. She adorns her bed with a bedspread printed with bouquets of green flowers, made from a fabric that I can't stand. It's a kind of fuzzy polyester that irritates my skin with the slightest rubbing. She insists on using it. We always have to throw it off the bed where it becomes a mound on the floor while we make love. Except for using that bedspread, Lucía doesn't do anything that goes against my taste. Since the bedspread is there and since there are two reasons for not keeping quiet, I speak.

I give Lucía all the details regarding the conflict between the trespassing family, Mr. Carpato and myself. "First, you have to consider your position in all this," Lucía tells me. "You are not the owner of the building. You are an employee of the owner. In that sense you are equidistant between the possessor and the dispossessed."

Whenever Lucía uses a word like "equidistant" I know that it doesn't bode well. I'm fairly certain that soon to follow is a flood of phrases like: "The bed is my only temple," phrases that, like her bed, are covered in a material that gives me an unbearable rash.

Lucía believes that the poor are good because they are poor and the rich are bad because they are rich. She doesn't realize that all people are the same.

"I saw their clothes hanging from the upper-story windows," I tell her. "They looked like they were made of silk, white and satiny. They were very shiny,"

"You feel guilty for having to evict them," Lucía says

"so you invent mysterious clothing. Of course, if instead of being needy poor people they're mysterious strangers it's much easier to throw them out."

"They left scarcely a crack in the doorway. I couldn't see what kind of people they were."

"Whoever needs to occupy a house in disrepair is, from the get-go, a poor wretch."

"Nevertheless, from the get-go they laughed it up, and furthermore, the house, the building, is not in disrepair; it's still under construction."

What is seduction? I once read something on the subject. It's not, without a doubt, what I exercise over Lucía. I've somehow, unknown to me, now managed to quiet her down and get her into bed. Between our arguments and our jumping into the sack there are no intervening acts or words. We give in to sex without realizing it.

It's true, I'm anxious about the fact that I have to throw them out of the building. But it's not true that I'm willing to fool myself over it. The clothes I saw hanging from the upper floors looked more like silk or satin than any other kind of fabric. And the red stain, which I didn't mention to Lucía because who knows what she'd come at me with, was not a deception but a red stain. I am anxious though. Otherwise, I wouldn't be spending the night with Lucía like I am, since there's no longer a need to, and loneliness has ceased to be a problem.

Lying next to Lucía at this hour is what she would call a novel situation. She can't say it because she's asleep.

I'm trying to sleep. It's actually strange that I can't. The bedspread is bunched on the floor in the corner of the room.

After years and years, can a fixed stare cause erosion on the ceiling? If for centuries men took turns, one generation after the next, staring at the same spot on the ceiling . . . would they not erode it away? Time would erode it first. Time is much more powerful than the stares of men.

For example, nighttime is one of the more polished forms of time. ("Polished forms" is an expression borrowed from Lucía). The night is pure time. This night, for example, here in this room now, is the same kind of night that would infiltrate the three-story walk-up on Larrea Street where I spent my childhood. I remember it well because once when I was ten I was climbing the stairs on a night just like this and I saw, on the second floor, a glow-in-the-dark poster of Woody Woodpecker on the door of apartment 12 announcing a birthday party. It's a nice custom, putting up a children's poster with the word "Welcome." At my house, on my birthday, we hung up a poster like that.

When God decided to smite the Egyptians with a deadly plague because they wouldn't let His people go, he told the Jews to make a mark on the doors of their homes so that he would know where not to mete out punishment.

Posters of Woody Woodpecker or Bozo the Clown hung out on birthdays are the sign, on the door of the home, that on that day someone in that house is happy; on that day, the small human inhabitant of the house belongs to the world of happiness. That poster, on that day, is a plea to God. It is implored of God—who is sparing with His benevolence and generous with punishment—that on that day the marked house not be visited with sadness or death. I wonder what kind of poster has been placed at the doorway by the family that shouldn't be living there.

Great, I'm wide-awake, and when I can't get to sleep I'm terrible. I begin to think of all kinds of things.

Like Lucía when she tries to make me believe that she's "delirious," saying that her own words are "a delirium."

I don't dare glance at the alarm clock, but at six o'clock I'm going to wake up or get up and carry out my task at the unfinished building at Tucumán and Uriburu, along Uriburu. (Uriburu takes its name from the Paraguayan bird, the uriburu).

Six in the morning is a ghastly hour for anyone. You can't even have breakfast at that time. Nevertheless, the neighborhood is already up and bustling.

One would think people are paid hundreds of thousands of dollars to get up at this ridiculous hour of the morning, but no: those who get up at six o'clock tend to be the ones who make the least amount of money.

The fourth corner, along the same sidewalk as the property, is occupied by a bar and a newspaper kiosk. The kiosk is run by Tuchito, the son of old man Tucho, the former newspaper vendor.

Tuchito is hunchbacked and greets me as if he were older than I. Without uttering a word I return his greeting with a wave of my hand. Within a few strides of the building I halt and retrace my steps.

"What's up, Tuchito?" I ask as a greeting to him.

"Would you like the *Morning News*?" he replies.

"Nah, that's okay. Listen, have you seen the guy who lives at that construction site?"

I believe "construction site" is the perfect term to describe the property.

"No," Tuchito tells me, "As far as seeing goes, I've never seen him. But I know a family is living there."

"Yeah. They don't buy the newspaper?"

Tuchito laughs.

"No. I don't think they're the kind of folks that read the newspaper. Like I said, see 'em, I've never seen 'em. Not in the deli or the bakery. What are they eating in there? Sand?"

"Perhaps. Or the damp air. Who knows?"

"Alright," Tuchito insists, "can I get you the *Morning News*?"

"Alright," I repeat, "I'll take it."

"Here you go." Tuchito says, taking my money and handing me the paper. "Anyway, if you don't read it you can use it to cover your head. Looks like we're in for a good one."

He's right. The early morning darkness has given way to some enormous black rain clouds. I've never used an umbrella, so fat chance I'm going to cover my head with a newspaper.

Regrettably, nothing detains me and I arrive at the opening in the brick wall. The coins Tuchito gave me in change are jingling in the pocket of my corduroy pants. My armpits are drenched in sweat. Today's the day they're going to have to vacate the premises.

I clap my hands and shout: "Hey, you there in the house."

It's so annoying that there's no doorbell.

This time the answer is muted yet forceful. Slinking

through the opening I see a bare leg, coppery or olive-skinned, that ends in a white knee sock and a tennis shoe. Then comes an arm belonging to the same person, the same striking color as the leg. Finally, half a face and the long, wild flowing hair of an adolescent girl, and a pair of breasts that barely fit through the narrow opening.

She's standing in front of me dressed in a sort of long T-shirt or tunic that, as "mysterious" as it may seem to Lucía, is also made from silk or satin, which compels me to glance upward and see if the same garments as yesterday are still hanging there. There's only one, and it's not the one with the red stain.

"My papa says for you to come in," the girl announces.

I'm afraid to go in, for the stench. As a way to turn down the invitation I decide to establish a position of authority.

"Tell your papa that he is not the owner of the house, that he cannot invite me in and that he must leave."

"Tell him yourself," the girl snaps back. She slips back inside through the opening just as the first drop of rain falls.

The father appears through the opening, much faster than his daughter. A loud thunderclap leaves us staring at one another in silence.

He's short and stout. I'm almost a full head taller than he. The rainfall brings with it a kind of clarity. I see his coppery or olive-toned face, the same skin as his daughter, and the same white silk or satin clothes too. With a completely unabashed gesture, like a lewd greeting, he takes his hand and adjusts the crotch of his loose-fitting white trousers. The rain comes down harder.

"Are you coming in or are we going to get soaked?"

"You have to leave," I say.

"Yes," he says. "We'll leave, but first I have to speak with you."

"No," I reply. "There's nothing to be said. You have to get out today. If you don't, I'll have the police throw you out."

"If the police could throw me out, you wouldn't have come alone."

The rain has now turned into a downpour. The newspaper is melting in my hand so I toss it.

Without warning, the short stout man grabs my arm and pulls me toward the opening. I try to break free, but he has an exceptionally strong grip on my sleeve and wrist, and in an instant I'm passing through the opening. Hopefully Tuchito is watching all this.

I scrape my nose and feel a burning sensation and blood, but the worst part is the stench.

"I assume you can't stand the smell," the man says to me as he hastily drags me toward a door leading to a staircase. On the way, I step on what appears to be rotting food, in particular vegetables.

The staircase leads to the basement, where it's much easier to breathe.

"You can breathe now," he tells me.

Even though I've been taken semi-prisoner in a dark basement I try to see things as Lucía would.

I shouldn't forget: this is a homeless family like so many others surviving in big cities without a roof over their heads or food on the table.

The daughter and someone who must be the wife burst

into the basement with lanterns that reek of fuel. The woman can't be more than forty and on her face she carries the expression of a big-screen prostitute.

The thunderstorm is horrendous and can be heard so loudly in the basement that for a moment I forget the situation I'm in and say: "Man, it's really raining."

"Rain," the man says in a mocking tone. "You people don't know what rain is."

"I guess not," I say, unsure if I'm trying to ingratiate myself with him. "I can't imagine what it would be like without a roof for protection."

"No, you can't imagine, but I don't mean that. I'm talking about when the roof isn't enough. I'm not talking about types of roofs. I'm talking about types of rain."

The dim light, to which my eyes have now adjusted, allows me to clearly see the basement, and just as clearly the faces of its occupants.

The woman's face, that the darkness might have distorted, is in the light still that of a prototypical prostitute. The girl's is attractive and cynical. And the man's, though he's not more than forty, is ancient and has a strange solemnity about it as if he had been cast in bronze—austere, the face of a villain.

I already know what Lucía's going to say when I tell her that these people's skin was olive or copper-toned. She'll say that I'm afraid of being racist and of evicting dark-skinned people, and therefore I invent a skin color for my victims so that they are more mysterious than needy. Then again, Lucía has not been nor will she ever be here.

Even if she were here, it would be she who would be determined to turn a blind eye to the truth before her.

Never have I seen skin like that before.

Why don't I try to hit this guy while he's speaking and make a break for the opening? Or why don't I simply stand up and announce that I'm leaving?

Because I know he'll stop me. He forced me inside and he won't let me leave until I've listened to him. If, when I consider our conversation to be over, he still doesn't let me leave, then I will indeed defend myself and attempt to escape as best I can.

"It's silly," he tells me. "You have to sign that document for me stating that I left of my own free will, without causing any damages, and provide a recommendation for someone to rent a place to me. It's that document right over there."

He points to a small metallic box the size of a large dictionary.

"If you and your family leave this very day," I say, "I don't believe Mr. Carpato will object to signing something for you."

"I want you to sign it, and now," the man states.

The two women look at me.

"I don't have the authority," I say to him.

"As far as I'm concerned you do," the man says. "You are the one sent by him to evict us."

"But he's the one who gives the orders."

"And you're the one who obeys."

"May I see the document?"

"Not yet," says the man.

He stands, leaves the basement, and comes back with a green bottle that appears to be filled with wine. As the door opens, my nose, which had become accustomed to the dank yet mild odor of the basement, gets a whiff of the putrid stench that accompanies him on his return.

The man picks up the bottle and pours the wine directly into his mouth, spilling it all over himself as he empties the contents. The red stains adorn his white clothing.

The woman, who must be his wife and mother of the daughter, kneels before him and pulls down his pants. It's high time I get out of here.

The woman is kissing him down there, he's fondling his daughter, and the basement door won't open. The handle is missing.

"Open the door!" I scream.

The man's hand is snaking around beneath his daughter's tunic while she's got her eyes fixed on me.

"You can watch," the man says to me. "You're welcome to stay."

"Open this door for me!" I shout again.

I kick the door, barely managing to get a dull thud out of it.

The man, immune to the racket I'm making, is lying on top of his daughter lifting her tunic while the wife kisses him on the back and buttocks.

The girl never stops staring at me, now, clearly, silently pleading for help. There's a bottle. I can break it and try to kill him.

But I hardly manage to yell, "Open this door!"

As if this were the first time he heard me, he interrupts his bacchanal and walks toward the table where the metallic box is. He opens the box like one opens a book. He takes the door handle from inside it.

"Come sign," he says to me.

I don't know why, but I truly believe that if I sign he'll let me go.

The girl bites her lower lip, looking at me as if I could do something.

I walk toward the table. The man places the door handle inside the metallic box on top of what appears to be a printed manuscript.

It won't be a sin of haughtiness or insanity if I allow myself to surmise that it's written in Aramaic.

I recognize the Aramaic words because when Lucía proposed to me I asked a rabbi to show and read to me the *ketubah*, the Jewish marriage contract that to this day continues to be written in Aramaic.

Trying to take in all this lunacy, I barely manage to utter: "Let me go."

"Sign first," he says.

There's no pencil, pen, nothing. He notices my apprehension. I can't believe he's going to pull a pen out from under his robes.

He seizes my arm.

"Sign with your thumb. Press your thumb here," he instructs.

"And then you'll let me go?"

The man takes the door handle and places it in my right hand.

"Of course," he tells me.

He takes my left hand and directs it toward the printed paper.

Out of pain, I struck him in the face with the door handle.

Just now, an instant afterward, I realize the source of the pain.

He slammed the metallic lid on my left hand. I catch a glimpse of my own blood drops on the first page of the manuscript.

The man gets up. The blow I delivered had dropped him to the floor.

I look at my wounded hand and advance with the handle toward the door.

The three of them watch me. The door opens.

I hold my breath and head toward where I believe the opening to be. I search haphazardly, there's no light coming in.

Finally, I hear drops of water splashing on the ground. They're coming from outside. I'm free.

Lucía says I can't accept people who are different. She says that incest inside a ten-room mansion is not the same as in a shelter where everyone is forced to eat, bathe, and sleep together. She says that in the case of the property at Tucumán and Uriburu they are all victims of incest, while in a mansion they would be guilty of it. She says something to me about upbringing that frankly I don't understand.

I tell her that the girl is the victim and the father is guilty.

She says I'm wrong, that surely the man was abused as a child and doesn't know any better.

I tell her that I saw the whole thing and that she doesn't know what the hell she's talking about.

She gets mad. She tells me that if we all needed to see things to be able to understand them there'd be no such thing as historians.

I tell her that historians aren't the ones who understand things, rather the ones who repeat them. She says I'm the one who doesn't understand because I freaked out when I saw a text in Aramaic in the hands of these people when I should know that, in Once, they could very easily have found a discarded or lost *ketubah*. I tell her that it wasn't a *ketubah*. I know good and well what a *ketubah* is.

She says that they easily could have stolen the metallic box from a rabbi believing it to be valuable or filled with jewels, and they wound up with a text in Aramaic that's of no use whatsoever to them.

I tell her yes, that's entirely possible.

Emboldened, she keeps giving explanations and says that my hand injury (which, I have to admit, Lucía bandaged properly) is due to the fact that I occupied a position in the struggle between the classes. It's due to the fact that the dispossessed blindly attacked a representative of the possessors. Now I get pissed off. Really, really pissed off. I insult her. I insult her in the worst way.

My anger comes in waves. At times it seems to have calmed down and then from behind comes a new mass of water with its foaming crest.

In a moment of calmness I tell her that she's insensitive, that she has no idea what pain is. The anger washes over me again and I tell her that I will never have kids with her, that she'll be dried up and alone like a solitary old fruitless tree.

My last insult is too violent even for me, so I storm out slamming the door shut behind me. I'm madder at myself than at her, and then I get mad at her for having made me so mad.

I have to get away from Pacheco de Melo Street.

Now that I'm on Bartolomé Mitre, walking toward my house and trying to forget the day, I start thinking. I think about my life and I think that with that insult I insulted myself as well. I'll never have descendants either.

I can't sleep. It's as if the squatter family poisoned me. I think about dying without ever having children and the image of the girl biting her lower lip pops into my mind.

It's very strange, because I want to rescue the girl as if she were my own daughter, but once I rescue her, my imagination doesn't let me treat her like a daughter.

I marry her.

All men have the same two thought processes: the first is where we are able to guide our thoughts; and the other is when the thought takes over and continues by itself.

When I think about rescuing her as a daughter, I tell her my hand hurts (it is seriously hurting, a lot); and when the thought continues by itself, she, in order to ease my pain, takes my hand and sucks it.

When my thoughts get away from me like that I forget about the pain and I have to make an effort to return to my senses and feel the pain in my hand.

I say to myself: "What an idiot, why do I want to remember the pain in my hand?"

And I answer: "No, I'm not such an idiot; I know the

pain is real, my hand will heal and the pain will pass; meanwhile this is a pernicious daydream and who knows where it will lead me."

In contrast to progressive thinkers like Lucía, for whom it's always better to go with the flow, I like to know where I'm headed.

Although I try to fall asleep—early tomorrow I should go see Mr. Carpato and inform him of the situation—I can't stop seeing the girl in my mind with her teeth sunk into her lip, like a kitten.

Marga shoots me a triumphant look, as if she knew that because of her I've stopped using Bach Flower remedies.

I'm seated with my good hand resting on top of the bandaged one. The scent of the mint gum that Marga is chewing wafts my way.

Marga is intimidating; although she arouses me, I'd never go to bed with her. The authority of her body frightens me a little.

I don't feel weak or cowardly for that; every man has the right to be turned on by a certain type woman and to sleep with whomever he pleases.

I'm convinced that Mr. Carpato and Marga are lovers. However, I find it impossible to imagine Mr. Carpato in bed with anyone. Mr. Carpato gives the impression of being too majestic for sex. He's too imposing to allow himself to reveal a grimace of relief.

Pomesano's voice comes over the intercom.

"Tell him to come in"

"You can go on in, Blot," Marga says to me.

Mr. Carpato, his bald head and immense body, light-colored suit and matching tie; and Pomesano, his hair stylishly long and his nose even longer but not so stylish, looking like the poor devil he is, are seated with some papers in front of them and I can tell from the way they're both staring at me that they want me to have a look.

"You couldn't throw them out. Right, Blot?"

I nod affirmatively.

"Not even using social psychology?" he jokes.

The corners of Pomesano's mouth start to rise to form a smile but Mr. Carpato cuts him short with a steely glare in his direction.

"You're not to blame, Blot," he remarks with sincerity. "These guys are professionals."

I don't know to what he is referring exactly. If he's talking about the squatters, I would like to clarify that they're not guys, rather two women and a man. But I can't bring myself to make clarifications.

Mr. Carpato hands me the file that he was looking at with Pomesano.

"Take a look at this," he says. "This family is letting itself be used."

I hesitate to take the file. I can't get yesterday's experience out of my mind. Now all documents seem evil and dangerous to me.

"What happened to your hand?" Mr. Carpato finally asks.

I can't think of anything to make up, so I tell him energetically: "The truth: I got in a fight with my girlfriend and I slammed the door as I stormed out. Would you believe I caught my hand in it?"

Mr. Carpato nods and Pomesano, who due to the pre-

vious silent reprimand understands that he should be nice
to me, says:

"Well . . . when you're upset, you do all kinds of things."

I nod and stick my face in the file, but I don't read it.

I'm thinking that Mr. Carpato didn't believe me.
What's more, I think that he already knew how I hurt my
hand and he asked because he assumed he shouldn't have
known. I think my lie must have amused him and he's
taking pity on me. He observes me like he believes I'm
reading, so I'd better read.

The file contains a detailed report on the business
maneuverings of the competition, the empire of Lubrano
Properties.

It seems that Mr. Lubrano is in the practice of placing
families of squatters in the unfinished properties of his
competitors. In this way he's able to have an adverse effect
on them and, in the same neighborhood and the same
market climate, he can sell his properties more quickly.

The report states that the families, honest-to-goodness
homeless people, are in collusion with Mr. Lubrano. In
addition to that precarious roof over their heads, which
for them means everything, they also receive a sum of
money.

"The money part seems odd," I say raising my eyes.
"Because these people live in filth and eat garbage."

"But they drink nice wine," Mr. Carpato says.

I can't bring myself to contradict him.

"The report generalizes," says Mr. Carpato, "but it is
based exclusively on the family that you must evict."

"And why does it generalize?" I ask just to say
something.

"How should I know," he replies. "I paid a lot of money for this investigation and they must have thought they should provide me with more material. Whatever the case may be, those people, the ones living in the property on Tucumán and Uriburu, have done the same thing at other properties. Evicting them with the police is no good for business. The legal proceedings can go on for years, and by that time Lubrano has made all the sales he needs to.

"Can we sue Lubrano?" I ask.

"No," Pomesano pipes in. "There's no proof."

"Blot," Mr. Carpato says, "you've seen that social psychology doesn't get results. They have to be killed."

Since I don't respond, Mr. Carpato opens a desk drawer, takes out a blueprint, and hands it to me. I'm still holding the files in my hands.

"Understand, Blot, that for something like this I can't send poor Pomesano," says Mr. Carpato as if Pomesano weren't there.

"Why not?" I ask in earnest.

"Because poor Pomesano," Mr. Carpato answers, "has already carried out similar tasks for me and with such dreadful skill that he's ended up at police headquarters on more than one occasion. As soon as the police see him, we'll be in real trouble."

"Mr. Carpato," I exclaim dumbfounded, "who is it that you're going to kill."

Mr. Carpato rearranges my entire sentence.

"'You,' no. We are going to kill. We are going to kill the family, that by my express orders, you were supposed to evict."

"But there are two women," I say.

"I know that," Mr. Carpato tells me, "and one man."

"I'm not going to kill anyone," I say.

"No, you're not going to execute anyone," Mr. Carpato says. "I'm showing you these blueprints so that you see where we can hide the bodies."

"Look," he tells me spreading the plans out on the desktop, upon my inability and refusal to take them from him. "This is the property."

It's the building plans.

Behind the property there's an empty lot. Next to it there's a synagogue, the front of which faces Pasteur Street. It occurs to me that, perhaps, by way of some secret passageway, the man entered the synagogue and stole the metallic box with the Aramaic manuscript. Except for the secret passageway, it seems plausible that the man had stolen the metallic box from the synagogue next door.

"The basement is dug into the empty lot," Mr. Carpato says. "There's a crawlspace one-meter wide between the basement wall and the adjoining lot. That dirt wall is our first option for burying the bodies wrapped in garbage bags.

"Mr. Carpato," I say to him, "you cannot kill them." There's a young girl. Perhaps the two of them are bad news, they work for Lubrano, but the girl's not even fourteen years old. I assure you the girl has nothing to do with it." (She's a virgin! I almost shout out).

"Oh, you know them well," Carpato remarks. "They know you. We can use that, Blot. The other option is the basement air vent. It's a hole that runs from the basement ceiling outside to the ground level of the vacant lot. We were thinking of putting a grate over it and cementing it closed. Right now it's nothing more than a hole covered by a metallic cap with a handle on it. That's the other option. What do you think?"

"Mr. Carpato, listen to me, please. The girl's got nothing to do with it."

"I always listen to you, Blot. Whether or not I follow your advice is altogether another story."

Pomesano's about to crack a smile, but he holds back.

"Pomesano," orders Mr. Carpato, "go make us some tea."

I note that Pomesano has been drastically demoted in status.

"I'm listening, Blot."

"Mr. Carpato," I tell him, "the girl is innocent. I assure you."

"Look, Blot," Mr. Carpato says to me. "I don't believe that the girl is innocent. But I have yet to make a final decision. You know that I can take her out, right?"

"Yes," I say, imagining the infinite vastness of the Carpato empire.

"But let's do the following," Mr. Carpato tells me. "If you really discover that the girl is innocent, which I truly doubt, but if you guarantee me that, work it out with her so that, together with her family, she gets out of there. Find a way to explain to her that if not, her parents, who are not innocent, will die. Work it out, Blot, in a way that can't be recorded and they can't claim it was a threat. If you bring me the proof tomorrow that the girl is innocent and of your arrangement with her, we'll see what we do then. If not, the day after tomorrow, I will kill them. Now beat it, Blot, before that imbecile Pomesano finishes making the tea."

Lucía says she wants to come with me.

I went back to beg forgiveness and ended up staying.

One thing's for certain, when I stayed up all night before the meeting with Carpato I spent it having paternal and not so paternal visions of the girl, which led to me feeling fairly randy in spite of all the trouble and Mr. Carpato's sinister plan.

It's not like I went back to Lucía just because I was horny. I truly went back to ask for her forgiveness, but if I hadn't been horny I wouldn't have stayed.

I have no idea if Lucía forgave me, or whether she was feeling just as horny and I was her last resort.

I told her absolutely not. I won't let you come with me to the building on Uriburu. She said that after what's happened I need company.

Her argument is that she understands these people better than anyone. I tell her that she doesn't even know what kind of people they are.

"I know all too well, they're people with problems," she responds. "People with no resources and a lot of problems," she insists.

I can't hush her up with a romp under the sheets because we just did that.

I tell her that it's my job and to keep out of it.

"Your job is to sell properties, not to be an executioner," she asserts.

I tell her that I'm far more aware of that than she can imagine.

What I haven't told her, what this dumb-bunny dreamer doesn't know, is that my only purpose, my only motivation for going back to that damned building is to save the girl.

My life has completely changed in three days. The tranquility in which I grew close to Lucía over the years is now the best memory I have of the person I was a mere three days ago. Nothing or no one could make me return to that shambles of a building after what happened to me. And yet, here I go, of my own free will, or whatever you want to call it.

A poor girl made to suffer by being pinned under the body of a pervert. That poor girl, the same exuberant girl with the coppery—or olive-colored—skin all dressed in white clothing and with breasts that heave when they pass through the opening.

For God's sake, I'm heading up Bartolomé Mitre, and Uriburu Street, which begins once you cross Rivadavia, pulls me like a great force in a direction I shouldn't go. How can I stop this crazy ride and get back on track? Sarmiento Street, broad Corrientes Avenue, the dirty and discreet Lavalle, and finally Tucumán; the vertiginous Uriburu has brought me all the way up here.

It's ten o'clock in the morning.

Tuchito greets me good-naturedly even though I didn't buy a paper from him. She's standing in front of the building, next to the opening. I'm not the only one who thinks she looks strange. The passersby stare at her as they scurry along the sidewalk. I approach quickly.

"Let's go," I tell her.

She's biting her lower lip.

"Let's go," I repeat. "This is our chance to escape."

"Mama is very sick," she says. "You have to help me carry her."

"We'll come back with the police, with a doctor, but first let's get out of here. First we have to hide you, free you from the clutches of that . . ."

"I'm not budging from here without Mama."

"But your father's inside. He won't let us leave."

"Papa's not here. He got drunk and he must be sleeping it off somewhere. I'm here alone with Mama, she's really sick. Help me get her out of here."

"What's wrong with her?"

"She's had an asthma attack. A bad one."

She goes inside. I notice that there is no longer a fetid stench.

"Come on," she begs me.

I follow her in. Four lanterns light the room, which is now clean.

The foul odor is gone and the cement floor looks spacious and empty. The only things in the room are the four lanterns, a ten-liter container that must be filled with fuel and a red box of matches.

"Where's your mother?" I ask.

"In the basement. She must be feeling better if she's no longer coughing."

"Let's go have a look," I say.

"We have time," she replies. "Come."

She intends, by the signals she's giving me, for us to lie down together. She lifts her tunic and reveals her sex, which is unlike any I've ever seen in my life. When I was this girl's age, no girl would have shown me something like that. At any rate, I'm like a boy before the enormity of her dark beauty.

"Come," she tells me, completely undressing.

I blanket her with my body. I want to say something, but words fail me. Before I know it I'm inside her.

Paradoxically, possessing her helps me to gain self-control. I manage to separate myself and I take her by the shoulders.

"We can't do this," I tell her using one of Lucía's terms. "First, I have to help you solve your problems."

"What problems?" She asks.

"What problems!" I yell in astonishment, pointing at the empty room with one hand. "This doesn't seem like a problem to you?"

"I don't understand," she says.

"You're young," I say to her, stupidly adding: "You can still be happy."

"You people don't know what happiness is," she tells me confidently.

"'You people' who?" I ask in exasperation.

"You and your people," she replies equally confident.

"And you know what happiness is, do you?" I say angrily. "Who explained happiness to you, your father?"

"We know what happiness is. You all have forgotten. We are the last happy family. Come."

"No. Why did you ask me for help?" I say to her as if, only yesterday, she had actually spoken.

"I didn't ask for your help," she says sinking her teeth into her lip. "I asked you to please come back."

She pulls me close.

I've never been inside a woman like this.

As I'm melting into her, the father appears from behind. I can tell from the voice.

"I knew you people liked a clean floor. That's all it takes. A clean floor and that's it," he gloats in his strange accent, relishing the moment.

His daughter whispers something in my ear with the same accent.

While she's doing that, the man puts his hand on my back.

He presses me against his daughter. She's unperturbed, and even helps him to keep a hold on me. I try to break free. The daughter grips on to me and kisses me, he's behind me, and I'm trapped between the two of them. The man comes down on me. I just want to die.

"Good," he tells me. "You signed the contract and fulfilled your part of the bargain. I'll fulfill mine. We'll leave this instant."

I can't bear to look at him. The girl is no longer underneath my body.

I sit up and try to get dressed. I see the woman behind the basement door. She's packing a bag that seems to contain her belongings. The man walks toward her.

The girl is behind me, I don't know where exactly.

I remember the blow I dealt the man yesterday. I knocked him down with it. I could do it again. He's got his back to me now, going down the stairs into the basement.

I lunge at him and with all my strength drive my fist into the back of the neck. He topples down the stairs and collapses in a heap on top of his wife. I take the handle off the basement door and close it. I grab the fuel container, the matches, and a wick from one of the lanterns. I dash from the building and run for the vacant lot. It doesn't take me long to find the capped vent. I pour half the contents of the container down the basement vent. I hear their cries for mercy; both the man's and the woman's begging. I don't know where she's gone to. Next, I soak my tie, light it on fire and drop it down the hole.

Standing next to the air vent, I wait expectantly to hear the crackling of the flames. I put the wick in the spout of the container with the remaining fuel, light it and cram the whole thing down the vent. I hear noises and the violent stomping of feet as if they were trying with all their might to put out the flames that rise from the floor, creep along the walls, and fall from the ceiling. Finally, the first shriek.

I go back around to the front of the building. She's disappeared. But I can't believe who is here. It's Lucía. What's Lucía doing here? Clouds of black smoke billow from the opening in the building.

"Lucía," I shout. "What the fuck are you doing here?"

"I came to help you," she says. "What's going on?"

"Nothing's going on," I tell her. "Why?"

"The place is burning down!" she screams.

"Nothing's burning!" I respond in a crazed voice.

"Look . . . there are flames!"

The first flames appear through the opening.

"Follow me and don't look back," I tell Lucía, crossing the street.

Lucía follows me but she's unable to keep from staring at the opening, where the flames are now swirling out.

"Follow me and don't look," I command her in a hoarse, infuriated murmur.

I can no longer see her. She's behind me, I think she's following me. I hear her shout.

Oh my God.

Lucía was struck by a bus.

She's lying there, under the tires of a bus, bleeding.

I regain my senses at the corner bar. Two policemen and Tuchito are slapping my face. Crowds of people gather in the street. Firemen.

They ask me if I knew Lucía. The question is tinged with sorrow and fear.

They ask me what happened inside the building. I tell them I don't know and that I should call Lucía's family, and my own.

They ask me to not leave the area, I'm a witness. I tell them that I wouldn't leave for anything in the world, and it's true. I burst into tears. They hand me a cell phone. I take the phone and head toward the commotion in the street.

My voice gets lost amongst those of the multitude of onlookers. My weeping was a cover. I don't feel anything in particular. I call Mr. Carpato.

Marga, diligently aware of the situation, puts me through.

"Mr. Carpato," I say, "It was no use. Not a one of them was worth saving. It's done. Am I in the clear?"

"Of course, Blot," Mr. Carpato tells me, discretely satisfied. "You've done more than was expected of you. Count on my protection."

I return to the bar and give the phone back to its owner. It's the first time I've used one of those devices. No cable or connections, it's like speaking with the great beyond.

I have a cup of coffee. I tell the policeman that I wish to speak with the fire chief, to help in any way I can, and I step out.

The fire chief informs me that they reached the basement where they discovered two charred bodies. He asks if I have any idea how the fire could have started.

They were odd people, I tell him. They used antique fuel-burning lamps and silk garments. They practiced strange rituals with fire around a metallic box.

"We've already found the box," the fire chief informs me. "It appears that a fuel container exploded next to them. That's how people get killed: with heaters, burners, and the like. We found the box you mentioned. Lieutenant Peralta has it. We had to spray it with the hose to cool it off. It was red hot! Guess what's inside? Papers!"

I dodge hoses and firemen to get to Lieutenant Peralta and explain to him that they stole the box from the synagogue next door.

"We should hand it over to the rabbi," I propose.

Lieutenant Peralta hesitates. I show him my ID and explain to him that I'm Jewish and that I can give it to the rabbi.

The convinced look on Lieutenant Peralta's face is even more absurd than my ploy, but he's still holding the box under his arm and with reservation insists, "I should check with the chief."

"The chief already authorized me to take it," I say.

The chief is busy with the fire, which miraculously didn't spread to the synagogue. They're trying to keep it from advancing toward Tucumán. Under the circumstances, Lieutenant Peralta reasons that it's not worth bothering him over a metallic box filled with incomprehensible papers and he relinquishes it to me.

Rabbi Nefret Yehuda reads Aramaic fluently. I've arrived at his temple, along with the destruction, like some kind of saving grace.

It's only here that I've been able to get some sleep. Nefret's been reading the text for more than five hours.

I doze off, but when I awake periodically he gives me updates. First he tells me:

"The metal is quite ancient. I've seen metals like this, but I can't say from what period it dates. If it were from the ancient Hebrews it should have finely engraved reliefs, but this is rather roughly hewn. On the other hand, I'm not familiar with the paper. I don't recognize the color or the texture and I'm astonished by how well preserved it is, because the text is clearly ancient. The ink is centuries old. The text doesn't appear to be written by scholars, rather by people who 'spoke' Aramaic."

While the Reb's getting keyed up, I'm overcome with drowsiness. As long as he reads and lets me take refuge in his temple I feel safe and sound. The noise has subsided

and the burned odor has neutralized into the surround-
ings. I was awoken once more for questioning, but they let
me answer right here. There must not have been anything
unnerving about the conversation because I fell right back
to sleep like a baby.

"It's the story of Sodom," bellows the rabbi, not waiting this time for me to wake up.

"It's like an atlas of Sodom!"

I glance at the clock. He's been reading nonstop for
twelve hours.

"It describes Sodom: 'Our beautiful S-d-m, its white
houses were of red roof sunrise in the docile land flow
wine honey and man need not work . . . We knew our
sisters and our mothers, our fathers we knew and they
us. Great pleasure we found in taking women and being
taken as women by men. We took the angel and we were
punished! Our S-d-m was lovely and lovely were the men
like tender reeds inside us and our girth was great in them
our brethren and fathers and He wished that we touch
not for in touching we were happy. And we took the angel
and the angel punished us!'"

"The sodomites attempted to do the abominable with
two angels," comments Nefret, agitated. "The Torah makes
a clear account of it. They attempted to 'know' two angels."

I think I must be dreaming this last part. I hope to not
wake up for a long while.

Between the head bobbing and the dozing on and off,
I've slept for twenty-seven straight hours.

Nefret hasn't stopped reading. The last time I awoke
his eyes were watering. Now, that it's impossible for me to
go back to sleep, his eyes are completely dry.

"Did all of them die next door?" he asks me.

"All of them," I lie.

"Listen," he tells me. "First they transcribe a paragraph from the Bible."

And He said: "I will certainly return unto thee when the season cometh round; and, lo, Sarah thy wife shall have a son." And Sarah heard in the tent door, which was behind him.

Now Abraham and Sarah were old, and well stricken in age; it had ceased to be with Sarah after the manner of women.

And Sarah laughed within herself, saying: "After I am waxed old shall I have pleasure, my lord being old also?"

And the Lord said unto Abraham: "Wherefore did Sarah laugh, saying: 'Can it be true that I am to bear a child now that I am old?' Is anything too hard for the Lord?"

"At the set time I will return unto thee, when the season cometh round, and Sarah shall have a son."

Then Sarah denied, saying: "I laughed not"; for she was afraid. And He said: "Nay; but thou didst laugh."

"Up to this point it's a textual transcription from the Bible, and here is their notation."

"Their?" I ask.

"The Sodomites," replies Nefret. "In their own sloppy style, sloppier even than the Bible. Listen:

Wherefore He did rebuke Sarah for laughing for thinking a smile He rebuked her being sparing in His

blessings and giving of punishment He did punish
the woman for thinking a smile We do laugh at Him
the first blood of our women whereupon their father
knows them does laugh at He who punishes.

"What do you think?" Nefret asks me.

"'Nay, but thou didst laugh.' How could the woman
not laugh if they tell her she'll have a child when she's a
hundred years old?"

"What do you think about the commentary of the
Sodomites?" Nefret insists.

"The Sodomites?"

"The natives of Sodom. Sodom and Gomorrah, the
cities destroyed by Hashem. According to the Bible, only
one family was saved: that of Lot; except for his wife
who was turned into a pillar of salt for having looked
back. That's the account according to the Torah. But this
Aramaic text (may the Lord quickly erase it from our
memory) speaks of another surviving family of Sodom, a
family that transmitted from one generation to the next
the customs of Sodom, up to the present day. As if today,
in this century, there were still living human vestiges of
the city destroyed by Hashem.

"There's a part of the text that they've made a concerted
effort to record," he says fearfully. "It concerns their laws,
the rules for enduring, for living on: if an entire people
need them in order to avoid dying out, imagine a single
family! In the beginning the manuscript must have been
a series of laws transmitted orally. It must have been
transcribed into written language in the 30th century of
our calendar, when Aramaic absorbed the other Semitic

languages. This family that authored the manuscript lived somewhere between the Euphrates and Asia Minor."

Nefret hesitates to read the next paragraph of the manuscript to me. I motion for him to proceed. I can't sleep anymore. He acknowledges and reads on:

And He slew our people because they were happy
    And He denied men from knowing happiness
    And He instructed Lot to flee and Lot fled without
warning us that death was approaching
    And fire rained down upon our heads
    The roofs offered no protection our hair was
scorched
    Children found no shelter
    And the family of Ephraim and Teo said
    let us hide ourselves beneath the earth
    Go not to their rescue
    let death come
    But let us save ourselves beneath the earth
    Let us save one family of Sodom
    We the last Sodomites do conspire
    against Him
    so that our lineage not expire
    We shall know one another amongst brothers
    and sisters brothers and brothers
    sisters and sisters parents shall know
    their daughters and sons and the
    sons shall know their mothers and the mothers
    their daughters and sons
    We shall clothe ourselves with the white raiment of
our happiness

We shall light our way with the water
that burns to not forget
that fire rained down upon our heads
We shall eat all that is putrid and vile
that His people do not eat
From our house fronts we shall hang
on the garments of the daughter the
first blood that the father wrenched from her
The Sodomite shall sow in his wife
If the firstborn is a girl she shall be preserved
If the second born is a girl she shall be slain
And so shall be slain all the girls born
who are not the first
All the males shall be preserved
If once twice three times a girl is born
the seed of the man is no good
The man shall acquire a guest
to impregnate the conserved daughter in
search of the male child of Sodom
Like the angels the guest shall be
known by the man and the woman
He shall be known like unto a woman and the man
of Sodom shall be treated
as a woman by the guest.

Nefret looks up, staring at me for several seconds
before I begin to vomit.

She is somewhere in the city. Will a rain of fire fall upon
this city someday or not? Buenos Aires is not Sodom. We

set ourselves ablaze slowly and imperceptibly. She wanders the city, taking me with her.

We are tied one to the other.

I have not spoken again with Pomesano or Mr. Carpato, nor will I ever. I will not be the one who places her in their hands.

Lucía would laugh if she knew that, since her death, I name her on a daily basis.

She would say that I "mythify" her, or use some other word of hers.

About the girl, I don't even know her name. I know that she belongs to the family of Teo and Ephraim.

I know that her skin and her customs are not our own, but perhaps she carries a son of mine in her womb.

If Mr. Carpato had seen my face when I was inside her just that once, then maybe, just once, he would ponder the extent of his empire.

Translated by Darrell B. Lockhart

Choco

José Eduardo Totah

IN SEPTEMBER of that year they appointed me manager of Human Resources and my wife announced that
we were going to have a baby. "The problem with you is
that you don't take risks," my mother had said right before
all of this happened, giving me a lecture with her little
cup of Green Hills tea in hand. She, like everyone else,
could not believe that they had promoted me so fast and
that Nora was going to have a baby. Executive and repro-
ductive success; I finally showed them all that there was
no challenge I couldn't meet.

JOSÉ EDUARDO TOTAH (1973–) Born in Buenos Aires, is
a journalist and professional musician. He has written articles
for *La Nación* and other national and international publications.
His stories have been published in the following collections:
Y otros cuentos (1995) and *La iniciación* (1998). His story "Otra
tormenta" ("Another storm") appears in the collection *Buenos
Aires no duerme* (1998) as one of the winners of the literary competition by the same name. He is currently working on a novel
titled *En tránsito* (In Transit).

Also that year I decided to distance myself once and for all from my pathetic childhood friends, and forced myself to meet people from the country club in Tortuguitas where I would go every weekend with Nora. I bought two Tombolini Italian suits for 3,000 pesos each and started jogging around the park on Tuesday and Thursday nights so I could fit into the pants.

The one activity in which I still crossed paths with my old friends was soccer on Saturdays. I had to return from Tortuguitas after lunch to meet with them at the fields that are located behind Club Atlanta, on Dorrego by the train tracks, at three-thirty sharp. They all came: Marcos, Dardo, Bruno, Lucho, Fabián, Jonás, Marino, Alberto, Toto, Teodoro, Julio, and some guy that no one ever figured out who invited, nor why on earth he was nicknamed Leche.

My new managerial outlook no longer tolerated those weekly rituals and it became clear just how depressing my teammates' lives were. Perhaps I was like them before the promotion, only I didn't realize it.

Marcos served as a corrupt public official in Morón; Dardo worked as a radiologist in a clinic in Avellaneda; Bruno was a lowly accountant in an office in Adrogué; Lucho ran the cash register in a rundown gift shop in Barrio Once; Fabián, a professional cocaine addict, was a psychoanalyst for some useless social organization and a compulsive divorcé (he's already been divorced three times, I believe, with four children from different marriages). Jonás was a forgotten trombonist who sat in the last row of the municipal orchestra of San Isidro. Marino was a freelance journalist for a hunting and fishing magazine. Alberto, an importer of wholesale pens, was always battling some kind of cancer. Toto, a writer of soccer stories, held on to the everlasting hope of winning an award, no matter how much we told him that serious literature, and above all the jurors of these contests, don't give a damn about anything that has to do with soccer. "Intellectuals hate the sport and won't even read your stories," said Leche, whose age was so indeterminable that he could have been anywhere from 15 to 35 years old. Now I don't remember what Teodoro, Julio, or our dear friend Leche did, but I can assure you they weren't rocket scientists on the brink of saving the planet.

Anyway I didn't write all this to tell you how pitiful my friends were, or how desperate I was to stop playing with them, but rather to talk about Choco.

Choco didn't teach me anything in particular; he wasn't a light that illuminated my way, not even a point of reference, much less a symbol of my new corporate life. Quite the opposite. He was, simply, the employee who took care of the fields and attended the locker rooms. But he was also, or at least I now think he was, the guy that saved my life. A little while ago, while looking him up on the Internet, I discovered that he was one of the toughest defenders in the history of Chacarita and perhaps the best number two that this country has ever seen.

Now retired, unemployed, and almost totally destitute, he had to take a job as caretaker of the property adjacent to Club Atlanta and, of course, had to conceal his affiliation with Chacarita, Atlanta's long-standing rival. If the *barra brava*, those Atlanta hooligans from Villa Crespo that stopped there on Saturdays to drink beer, had been aware of Choco's true colors, they probably would have killed him right then and there.

Choco spent most of his time drinking *mate* in a cage in the locker room, where he stored the soap and towels that he sold for two pesos. He was very dark-skinned, with black curls all over his head, and wore flip-flops, even in winter. He must have been about sixty-five, but his real age, like Leche's, could not be determined. On his left arm was a slightly faded tattoo with an inscription, in Portuguese, that said: "Barra da Tijuca '66."

He was also responsible for enforcing the schedule of the field rental.

We played from three-thirty to five and Choco would cut us off on the dot, like a bureaucrat who can't bear to see his subordinates sitting around doing nothing.

The scene would be brutally repeated every Saturday. Right in the heat of the game, when our legs are tensed and ready to attack and the goals are shouted more out of anger than anything else, Choco would appear ambling along with the assurance of someone who carried the full weight of the law. I was the first to see him coming, limping a bit on his right leg, engrossed in his own battles won or lost, with a silver whistle hanging around his neck like a referee. He seemed very satisfied with his role.

At five o'clock sharp the sound of the whistle marked the end of the Saturday game, and no amount of complaining could have changed that. We'd hurl insults at him repeatedly, begging him to let us have five more minutes: "What's it going to cost you, Choco? We've been coming here for a thousand years, it's no skin off your back, don't be a son of a bitch, come on." But the

guy would strut onto the field like a feudal lord in his
domain, call for the ball, and decree that the fun, what
was perhaps the highlight of the week for many of us, had
ended. He was Saturday's executioner. I still remember
the sound of his whistle. In this hour and a half, our lives
were no longer depressing: Marcos attained the status of
congressman, Dardo became a big shot in the medical
world, Alberto made the deal of the century and beat his
cancer, Fabián stopped divorcing, Marino won the Pulit-
zer, and Toto finally convinced a jury of notables that they
should award him a prize for one of his soccer stories.

The difference is that I no longer needed that hour and
a half to be successful. I had already become a manager.
What more could I want? My annual bonus was more
money than all of my friends together could earn in one
year. Choco was no executioner; he was only the caretaker
of the soccer fields that are behind Atlanta. For some reason that I still don't understand, I liked to imagine him
as a holy man executing his little rituals: arranging the
soaps and towels in his cage in the locker room, decreeing
the end of the hour on each of the fields, and taking the
bus every night at eleven thirty to return to a lonely little
house somewhere. Let's be honest: someone like me, at
the top of his career, would not usually concern himself
about a guy like Choco. But one time I stayed to visit with
Liz, the receptionist, and, without showing too much
interest, I casually asked about him. Apparently, even she
didn't know about his past history playing for Chacarita
(the secret was well guarded), but she knew that Choco
lived alone, that he had played in Russia, Germany, and
Brazil, that he had gotten a taste of the good life of the

greatest, most elite players—the long nights of drinking and women until dawn and the honors that come with the glory of being the most loved and admired defender of his time.

She also knew Choco had retired young and spent all of his fortune within a couple of years, showering gifts on everyone, like a king who sacrifices his gold to show his greatness. And that he had had a lot of women, but had only loved one, in some port in the south of Brazil, who left him with a son. And that the son, who was born deaf and dumb, had, at the age of eighteen, thrown himself under a train without anyone knowing why.

But I'm not going to beat around the bush anymore. What I have to tell you about Choco is what happened that September night.

It was Friday and I was heading to the country club on the *Panamericana*, as I did every Friday, relaxing to a Coltrane CD in my brand-new, recently delivered car, one of the perks granted to certain company executives.

It had been an interminable day, because we were closing the budget of the next fiscal year, and I stayed at the office until midnight, crunching numbers with the finance manager. Luckily, I had told Nora and my in-laws to wait for me in the house in Tortuguitas.

While I was driving in the fast lane that clear and warm night, I tried to think how to tell my friends that I wasn't going to play with them anymore, that I preferred to stay at the house in the country all weekend, that it was really too far to return just to go to Atlanta. I was also thinking about Choco.

Near Boulogne, my executive car started to cough and

I realized my mistake in ignoring the yellow indicator light of the gas tank, an infuriating sign that Nora had used the car all week without deigning to stop at a service station.

Cursing my wife and pounding on the steering wheel angry and frustrated, I managed to get off at the next exit, coasting to a halt practically right in front of the number 60 bus stop.

It was quarter to one and I felt like a complete idiot when I discovered that I had left my cell phone in the office.

What should a Human Resources manager do in a $60,000 car, at one o'clock in the morning at a deserted number 60 bus stop on the *Panamericana*, out of gas, and without a cell phone? The first thing that I did was lock the doors and consider my options. I remembered a management book I was reading that talked about "how to handle a risky situation while staying in control of your emotions in order to command leadership." I was a leader and the moment had arrived for me to demonstrate my managerial status beyond the limits of the office. I saw no public telephone to call for roadside assistance, and I couldn't just sit there all night. Then I noticed in the rearview mirror that the number 60 was approaching, lumbering along the nearly deserted freeway, slow and heavy. I got out of the car, making sure to lock up tight and stopped the bus.

In an instant, I felt that my safe little world—the company, Nora, the managerial benefits, the annual bonus, the friends, and everything else—was being held together by a thin thread. When I was younger, I used to take buses at all hours of the night to go out dancing. I was never scared of being out on the streets but that night I was terrified of everything and everybody.

The person who got on the number 60 bus wasn't me but a frightened deer, blinded by a gigantic light, cloaked in his Tombolini suit. I didn't even have change for the meter. "My car's stuck, it's that one, over there, I need to get to kilometer 38, near the country club, La Encantada, I have no cash, I have no gas, will you take me?" I begged the driver, almost stuttering. The man didn't say anything but answered with a friendly movement of his head for me to move to the back of the bus.

I thanked him and curled up into a ball on one of the single seats to the left. The bus was empty, except for some kids with their parents sitting in the back seats five across and some guy who was nodding off up front who, from time to time, would make small talk with the driver. What happened after that is a little fuzzy to me now. In the hospital they told me that we crashed in the 35th kilometer because of a pickup truck that was stalled with no lights in one of the lanes. I remember being shot in the air, swimming between glass and twisted metal, and being trapped between those irons, without the will to move a single muscle. What I do know is that someone took me by the arm and helped me out of the bus before it caught on fire. And that, in the midst of all the smoke and the confusion, I saw the defender fighting his last great battle, removing others from hell while he remained there, decreeing his own end. I could make out a glazed look, haughty but full of pride. The final point of a very tiring journey.

After that I blacked out, and in the days that followed I refused to listen to anything that had to do with the accident that night. I didn't read the newspaper and I expressly asked Nora not to talk to anyone about the matter. I didn't want to know nor did I want them to find out.

There is little to say about the rest of the story. I was kept under observation. ("Minor trauma and a few burns," they informed me. "You were very lucky," they said.) And in no time, I was back at work.

I went to visit my friends two Saturdays after the accident, at three-thirty at the field. In reality, I didn't go to meet up with them but rather to wait for Choco to appear in his flip-flops from afar, to kick us out at five.

I couldn't muster up the courage to go to his cage in the locker room. I preferred to stay seated in the wooden stands and follow the game as if it were a movie in black and white from the sixties, like one of those movies they used to show on Channel Eleven starring Yul Brynner and Stewart Granger, my first idols, who were already old when I was a boy.

This time they didn't seem so depressing; during this hour and a half they were truly my heroes. At ten after five my friends were still playing, completely oblivious to the time. Every so often they would look over to the side, expecting, perhaps longing for, the sound of the whistle.

I refused to stay any longer; I refused to keep on waiting. I got into the car, now with a full tank of gas, and vowed never to return.

Translated by Jill Gibian

The Place of Its Solitude

Luisa Valenzuela

All moon all year
all day all wind
comes by and passes on.
All blood arrives
at the place of its quietude.

(Books of Chilam-Balam)

THE ALTARS HAVE BEEN ERECTED in the country but the vapors reach us (those of us who live in the city, in the suburbs, those among us who believe that we can save ourselves). Those from the countryside have accepted their fate and are praying. Yet there's no visible motive for panic, only the usual shootings, police raids, custom-

LUISA VALENZUELA (1938–) Known for her forays into postmodernism, Valenzuela's novels and short stories portray Argentine life through humor, pathos, and irony. As one of the most important literary voices of her generation, Valenzuela knows the reality of exile and the shock of returning to her homeland post-dictatorship. She has received numerous honors including a Fulbright Fellowship to the University of Iowa's International Writing Program (1969), a Guggenheim Award (1983), and a Puterbaugh Fellowship (1995).

176

ary patrols. But they must be dimly aware that the end is at hand. So many things are so confused now that the abnormal is imitating the natural and vice versa. The sirens and the wind, for example: the police car sirens are like the howling of the wind, with an identical sound and an identical power of destruction.

To keep a better watch on the inhabitants of the houses, a type of siren is being used in the helicopters that is so high pitched and strident that it makes the roofs fly off. Luckily the government has not yet found the formula for controlling those who don't live in single houses or on the top floors of high buildings. And there are very few of these: since the electricity has been cut off nobody ventures beyond the third floor because of the danger of stairways, the hideout of malefactors.

We must add that as consolation many who lost their roofs have had them replaced with Plexiglas skylights, gifts of the government. Above all in rural areas, where the straw roofs frequently fall off not only because of the sirens but also because of windstorms. That's what they're like in the country: they put up with anything, even with remaining where they are and setting up altars and organizing prayer meetings when time and weather permit. They have little time for prayer, and bad weather. The southeast wind blows out their votive candles, and floods demand their constant attention to keep the livestock (goats, sheep, pigs, a very few cows, and a fair number of chickens) from drowning. Fortunately they haven't had the nerve to come to the city as they did seven years ago, during that historic drought, when thirsty men flocked to the cities in search of water, trampling the parched bodies of those who had died along the way. But the city was not a solution either because the city-dwellers didn't want them and drove them off with sticks like howling dogs, and they had to take refuge in the sea in water up to their waists, safe from the rocks hurled from the shore by those defending their bread, their drinking water, and their feeble dignity.

They aren't going to make the same mistake; even though this didn't happen here but in a neighboring country, it amounts to the same thing because while their individual memory is fragile their collective memory is enviable and comes to the surface to get them out of difficulties. Nonetheless we don't believe that the rebirth of religious sentiment will save them from what's happening now; it won't save them, but perhaps it will save us city-dwellers who know how to sniff the air for a breath of copal incense that reaches us from the interior. They have great difficulty importing copal incense and we may be the ones to reap the benefits. Exhaust gases permitting, we do our best to breathe great lungfuls of incense—we know it's useless—just in case. That's the way everything is now: we have nothing to fear yet we're afraid. This is the best of all possible worlds, as they keep reminding us over the radio, and the way other worlds will be; the country is on its way to the future, and secret agents of aberrant ideologies can do nothing to halt its march, the government says, so in order to survive we pretend that we believe it. Leaving aside those who are working in the underground—there are few of them—our one hint of rebellion is the surreptitious sniffing of the air in search of something that comes to us from the countryside and shows up our lack of faith.

I believe—I can't be sure, the subject is discussed fur-
tively—that in certain suburban districts of the city groups
of pilgrims are being formed to go to the interior to try to
understand—and to justify—this new mythical tendency.
We were never fervent believers and suddenly now we feel
the need to set up altars. There must be something behind
all this. In the café today with my friends—so you won't
think we're in really bad straits, I might mention that
friends can still get together in a café—very cautiously we
touched upon the subject (we must always be careful, since
the walls have ears) of what's going on in the interior. Has
excessive fear brought them back to a primitive search
for hope, or are they plotting something? Jorge suspects
that the copal has hallucinogenic powers and they deprive
themselves of many things in order to get it. It appears
that copal cannot be transported by mechanical means,
so it must come from Central America on the back of a
mule or a man. Relays to transport it have already been
organized and we might suspect that ammunition or at
least drugs or instructions arrive inside the bags of copal
bark, if it weren't for the fact that our customs officials are
so alert and clear-thinking. The local customs, of course,
don't permit copal to enter the cities. We don't want it
here either, although certain dissident intellectuals have
declared our city an area of psychological catastrophe. But
we have much more burning questions confronting us
and we can't waste time on speeches and lectures on so-
called metaphysics. Jorge says it's something much more
profound. Jorge says, Jorge says . . . All we can do in cafés
nowadays is talk, because in many of them we're no longer
allowed to write, even though we keep ordering food and

drink. They claim that they need the tables, but I suspect that those café owners who suppress the written word are really agents provocateurs. The idea started, I think, in the café at the corner of Paraguay and Pueyrredón, and spread through the city like a trail of lighted gunpowder. Now no writing is permitted in the cafés near the Mint, nor in some along the Avenida Rio Branco. In Pocitos yes, all the cafés allow writing and intellectuals gather there around 6:00 p.m. So long as it isn't a trap, as Jorge says, set up by the extremists, of course, since the government is above such machinations—in fact, above everyone in their helicopters, safeguarding the peace of the nation.

Nothing to fear. The escalation of violence only touches those who are looking for it, not us humble citizens who don't allow ourselves so much as a wry face or the least sign of discontent. (Of consternation yes, and there's good reason when they blow the roof off the house and sometimes the top of one's head as well, when they frisk us for arms in the street, or when the smell of copal becomes too intense and makes us feel like running to see what's up. Like running and running; acting absurdly is not always cowardice.)

We've finally become used to the smell of incense, which often competes with the smell of gunpowder, and now something else is coming our way: the distant sound of a flute. In the beginning we thought it was ultrasonic waves to break up demonstrations, but that wasn't it. The flute note is sustained, and to those not paying much attention it may sound like a lament; in reality it's a persistent melody that makes us lift our heads as in the old days when the roar of helicopters drew our attention. We have lost our capacity for amazement. We don't dance to that tune, nor do we break into a run when the patrols arrive from all directions and converge on top of us.

Sirens like the wind, flutes like ultrasonic notes to break up riots. It would appear that those in the interior have decided to borrow certain devices from the central power. At least that's what they're saying on the street, but it's never specified who those in the interior are: riff-raff, provincials, foreign agents, groups of armed guerril-las, anarchists, researchers. That flute sound coming on top of the smell of incense is just too much. We might speak of sensorial and ideological infiltration, if in some remote corner of our national being we didn't feel that it's for our own good—a form of redemption. And this vague sensation restores to us the luxury of being afraid. Well no, not fear expressed aloud as in other times. The fear now is behind closed doors, silent, barren, with a low vibration that emerges in fits of temper on the streets or conjugal violence at home.

We have our nightmares and they are always of torture even though the times are not right for these subtleties. In the past they could spend time applying the most refined methods to extract confessions, but now confessions have been consigned to oblivion: everyone is guilty now, so on to something else. In our anachronistic dreams we city people still cling to tortures, but those in the inte-rior don't dream or have nightmares: they've managed, we are told, to eliminate those hours of total surrender when the sleeper is at the mercy of his adversary. They fall into profound meditation for brief periods and keep nightmares at a distance; and the nightmares are limited to the urban community. But we shouldn't talk of fear. So little is known—we know the advantage of silence. What do those in the interior do, for example, in front of their altars? We don't believe that they pray to the god invoked so often by the government, or that they've discovered new gods or resurrected the old ones. It must be something less obvious. Bah. These things shouldn't worry us, we live within four walls (often without a roof or with a skylight)—men addicted to asphalt. If they want to burn themselves on incense, let them; if they want to lose their breath blowing into an Indian flute, let them. None of that interests us. None of that can save us. Perhaps only fear, a little fear that makes us see our urban selves clearly. But we should not allow ourselves to experience fear because with a breath of fear so many other things come our way: questioning, horror, doubt, dissent, disgust. Let those far away in the fields or in the mountains show a great interest in useless practices if they like. We can always take a boat and go away; they are anchored in one spot and that's why they sing psalms.

Our life is quiet enough. Every once in a while a friend disappears, or a neighbor is killed, or one of our children's schoolmates—or even our own children—falls into a trap, but that isn't as apocalyptic as it seems; on the contrary, it's rhythmic and organic. The escalation of violence—one dead every twenty-four hours, every twenty-one, every eighteen, every fifteen, every twelve—ought not to worry us. More people die in other parts of the world, as that deputy said moments before he was shot. More, perhaps, but nowhere so close at hand as here.

When the radio speaks of the peace that reigns (television has disappeared—no one wants to show his face), we know it's a plea for help. The speakers are aware that bombs await them at every corner; they arrive at the station with their faces concealed, so when they walk the streets as respectable citizens, no one will recognize them. No one knows who attacks the speakers—after all, they only read what others write. But where do they write it? Under police surveillance and in custody? That makes sense. Science fiction writers foresaw the present state of affairs years ago and the government is now trying to keep new prophecies from proliferating (although certain members of the government—the less imaginative among them—have suggested permitting freedom of action for the writers so as to lift interesting ideas from them). I don't go along with such maneuvers, which is why I've devised an ingenious system for writing in the dark. I keep my manuscripts in a place that only I know about; we'll see what happens. Meanwhile the government bombards us with optimistic slogans that I don't repeat because they're all so familiar, and this is our only source of culture. Despite which I continue to write and try to be law-abiding and not. . . .

Last night I heard a strange noise and immediately hid my manuscript. I don't remember what I was going to jot down; I suspect it's not important anymore. I'm glad I have quick reflexes because suddenly someone turned the master switch, all the lights came on, and a squad of police entered to search the house. It'll take poor Betsy a week to put everything back in order, to say nothing of what they broke or what they must have taken away. Gaspar can't console her, but at least nothing more serious has happened than the search. The police questioned them as to why they had taken me in as a boarder, but they gave an adequate explanation and luckily, as if by a miracle, they didn't find my little board painted in phosphorescent colors so that I can write in the dark. I don't know what would have happened to me, Betsy, and Gaspar if they'd found it all; my hiding place is ingenious and I wonder whether it might not be better to hide something more useful in it. Well, it's too late to change now; I have to keep walking along this path of ink and tell the story of the doorman. I was at a tenants' meeting and saw the single women mentally licking their chops when the new doorman was described: thirty-four years old and a bachelor. In the days that followed I saw him lavishing a lot of extra care on the bronze fittings at the main entrance and also reading a book while on duty. But I wasn't there when the police took him away. Rumor has it that he was an infiltrator from the interior. I know now that I should have talked with him, perhaps I would finally have understood something, untangled some of the threads of the plot. What are they doing in the interior, what are they after? I'd be hard put to say which of the single women in the building turned him in. They all look spiteful and perhaps have reason to, but are they all capable of running to the telephone and condemning someone out of spite? The radio gently urges us so often to inform, that they may even have felt they were doing their duty. I can now write all this down with a certain impunity, since I know I'm safe in my hiding place. That's why I can afford the luxury of writing a few stories. I even have the titles "The Best Shod," "Strange Things Happen Here," "Love of Animals," "The Gift of Words." They're only for me, but if we're lucky enough to survive all this, perhaps they'll bear witness to the truth. Anyway they console me. And with the way I've worked it out, I have no fear of playing their game or giving them ideas. I can even do away with the subterfuge of referring to myself in the plural or in the masculine. I can be myself. Only I want it known that even though I'm a little naive and sometimes given to fantasy, not everything I've recorded is false. Certain things are true: the sound of the flute, the smell of incense, the sirens. It's also true that strange things are happening in the interior of the country and that I'd like to make common cause with them. It's true that we are—I am—afraid.

I'm writing secretly, and to my relief I've just learned that those in the interior are also writing. By the light of the votive candles they're writing the book of our people. This is a form of illusion for us and also a condemnation: when a people writes for itself, it is dying out and nothing can be done about it.

Some make light of this bit of information: they say we city dwellers have no connection with people of the interior, that we all descend from immigrants. I don't see how coming from somewhere else can be a reason to be proud when the very air we breathe, the sky and the landscape when there's a drop of sky or landscape left, are impregnated with them—those who have always lived here and have nourished the earth with their bodies. And it's said that they're now writing the book and it's hoped that this task will take many long years. Their memory is eternal and they have to go a long way back in time to arrive at the origin of the myth, dust the cobwebs off it, and demythicize it (in order to restore to the truth its essence, to take off its disguise). They say that we'll still have time to go on living, to create new myths for them. The pragmatists are in the city, the idealists are far away. Where will they meet?

Meanwhile the persecutions grow more insidious. One can't go out in the street without seeing men in uniform breaking the law for the mere pleasure of laughing at those who must obey it.

Though I'm quiet these days, I go on jotting it all down in bold strokes (and at great risk) because it's the only form of freedom left. Others still make enormous efforts to believe the radio, which transmits information quite different from what is already public knowledge. This clever system of contradictory messages is designed to drive the population mad; to preserve my sanity, I write in the dark without being able to reread what I've written. At least I feel that I'm supported by my fellow country-men in the interior. I'm not writing a book like them, but it's something. Mine is a modest contribution and I hope it never gets into the hands of readers: I don't want to be discovered. Sometimes I return home so impressed by people who wander blindly in the streets—people who have been beaten, mutilated, bloodied, or crippled—that I can't even write. But that doesn't matter. Nothing would happen if I stopped writing. If the people in the inte-rior stopped writing—history would stop for us, disaster overcome us. They must have begun their story with the earliest times; one has to be patient. If they go on writing they may someday reach the present and overcome it, in all the meanings of the verb *to overcome:* leave it behind them, modify it, and with a little luck even improve it. It's a question of language.

Translated by Helen R. Lane

The Tourist

Carlos Chernov

> Kilimanjaro is a snow-covered mountain 19,710 feet high, and is said to the be the highest mountain in Africa. Its western summit is called the Masai "Ngaje Ngai," the House of God. Close to the western summit there is the dried and frozen carcass of a leopard. No one has explained what the leopard was seeking at that altitude.

—Ernest Hemmingway, *The Snows of Kilimanjaro*

ANDRÉS ARRIVED IN MENDOZA on the morning train and rented a room at a three-star hotel where he'd stayed on previous trips. After taking a quick shower he climbed into bed and spent the better part of the day there drifting in and out of sleep. When night fell he picked up the phone and ordered his dinner to be delivered to the room.

CARLOS CHERNOV (1953–) A physician by training dedicated to psychiatry and psychoanalysis, Chernov began writing at an early age, although he was first published in 1992. His unique style of writing juxtaposes a number of recurrent themes as he alternates between allegory, the fantastic, and science fiction. "The Tourist" comes from his second collection of stories *Amor propio* (2007).

After eating, he carefully cut three lines of cocaine on the glass-top night table and put the rest in the tobacco tin where he kept his stash. He alternated the cocaine with half a bottle of Reserva San Juan cognac while he watched television. At eleven o'clock he took a tranquilizer and a sleeping pill. He repeated the dosage at two-thirty in the morning and finally managed to fall asleep shortly thereafter.

The following day Andrés opened his backpack and spread the equipment he'd brought with him from Buenos Aires out on the bed, taking note of what he still needed to buy. He decided that this time he was not going to climb Aconcagua without the proper down-filled gloves with an adequate outer layer—he had suffered minor frostbite twice before. He would also need a good pair of double-layer, Koflach-type boots, ski poles, and all the provisions and butane canisters he could pack. He spent two days shopping for supplies. He bought the double-layer boots—leather on the inside with a hard plastic outer layer—from an Austrian who was returning home. The sale took place on the street, so they had to sit down on a bench in the plaza in order for Andrés to try them on. He struggled with the three pairs of long socks— one woolen—that were indispensable to withstand the temperatures of thirty to forty degrees below zero that awaited him on the mountain. When he finally managed to get them on he was practically out of breath. The Austrian stayed glued to his side as he tried out the boots. Andrés felt ridiculous walking around in heavy-duty hiking boots and shorts, dripping sweat from the hot, dry climate of Mendoza in January. Andrés had money to burn since before leaving Buenos Aires he had sold all his belongings—including an apartment and a car—and so he didn't need to acquire secondhand equipment, but he wouldn't have found boots of this caliber outside the used clothing trade that existed among the mountain climbers, many of them foreigners.

Andrés took the Expreso Uspallata minibus to Puente del Inca. On the ride up he was surrounded by backpacks, ski poles, and ice picks, but felt distanced from the atmosphere of excitement that engulfed the other climbers. After getting a room in a hostel—where he would stay just one night—he set out to hire the crew needed to transport his equipment by pack mule. While he was arranging a price—not caring that it was in dollars this time—Major Gutiérrez, the chief officer of the Puente del Inca garrison whom he knew from previous ascents, approached him. The major told him worriedly that several of his men were on the mountain attempting to bring down the bodies of two climbers. The casualties—as the major referred to them—had pitched a tent in the vicinity of the base camp known as Refugio Berlín, on the last stretch before the summit. One of them fell ill and was unable to continue on. The other began the descent in order to alert the rescue patrol, but later changed his mind, deciding to return and remain at his companion's side. Both men froze to death inside the tent. Andrés was choked up by the story. He was overcome by a feeling of pity for his mountaineering colleagues, in particular for the one who having been able to save himself refused to leave his friend alone. The intensity of his own reaction to the story took him by surprise. He was often criticized for his emotional coldness by people who knew him. He was forty years old, still single, and had no friends. Andrés reasoned that even though the only human company he kept was that of other mountain climbers, he had never really become very close to any of them, so he failed to understand why he was so emotional over this now. The thought of losing control alarmed him. He felt upset, anxious, nauseated. He imagined the nightmare scenario of coming across the tent where the self-sacrificing climber and his companion waited for someone to come rescue them. He also thought of how complicated bringing the stiff cadavers down from the summit of Aconcagua would be without the aid of the mules that were unable to climb to that altitude. Andrés was fascinated by the petrifaction of living substances, even if it were only from the effect of freezing. It was the idea that the organic could imitate an inorganic state. In that same spot, Puente del Inca, kids would submerge bunches of grapes in the river and in just a few weeks time pull them back out in a petrified state. They would sell them to the tourists as if they were relics found in Pompeii. Being a medical pathologist, Andrés made his living from the study of dead tissue. It had always seemed profoundly odd to him that the rounded shapes on cadavers—the back, the buttocks, the calves, and heels—could be transformed into completely flat surfaces by the marble top of the dissection table.

He set out at dawn wanting to reach the Horcones River before the water level rose above his waist and the freezing temperature and sharp, slippery rocks turned the crossing

into a difficult passage. Shortly after hitting the trail he
overcame a group decked out in expensive hiking gear.
Andrés always made the ascent alone. They greeted him
in English, and Andrés replied with a polite smile and
hiked on ahead. He knew the group's guide and was certain that he was already regaling his clients with tales of
the adventurous climber who had just passed them. The
guide would be telling them how Andrés had climbed the
sharp vertical cliffs of Yosemite Park in California, the
Ruwenzoris in Uganda and various other mountains in
Argentina, such as Fitz Roy and Cerro Torres. He would
conclude his story with the comment that Andrés had
completed several "eight-thousands" in the Himalayas; on
two occasions without an oxygen tank.

He traversed the Horcones River without incident
and taking the tobacco tin from his pocket he rewarded
himself with a portion of cocaine that he had to pinch
between his fingers to keep the wind from blowing it
away. He rubbed his gums vigorously with the powder
stuck to his fingertips. By midafternoon he reached Con-
fluencia where, much to his displeasure, he observed that
quite a few climbers already had made camp. He filled a
thermos with water from the stream, set up his one-man
igloo tent, and remained inside staring at the ceiling and
taking sedatives until he managed to fall asleep. He broke
camp in the morning and began the tedious hike across
Playa Grande, a monotonous expanse of rock that covered
some eleven kilometers. He became so bored and he was
carrying such a lightweight backpack that he had to resist
the urge to run. As a teenager he had spent his summers
in Bariloche with the instructors of the Club Andino. He

used to hike there with his pack filled with rocks, which was so heavy it would dig into his back and scrape the skin from his shoulders. The resulting lacerations left him with permanent scars. Nevertheless, Andrés convinced himself that there was no better endurance training for leg strength. His backpacks, needless to say, didn't last long since the bottoms would fall out under the weight of the heavy load.

Andrés was an only child whose parents sent him away to summer camp for three months from the time he was seven years old. Early in his teens he realized that his parents wanted him out of the house so that they could be alone. He always thought that they were too in love with one another. Andrés had a recurring dream in which he imagined the bodies of his parents stuck together like Siamese twins. Sometimes he dreamed they were joined at the legs; two torsos that shared one broad mermaid tail.

His father's reaction to his mother's death confirmed his theory of excessive love. Few things seemed as insufferable to Andrés as his father's weeping. When he wasn't crying over the loss of his wife, his father was blaming himself for not having saved her. He was a physician who considered himself to be a good clinician. His mother had died in less than a week, after falling victim to a sudden and devastating illness. His father had consulted the leading specialists who admitted her into intensive care on the first day of the illness. Yet, he reproached himself as if he had been truly negligent. His father stopped working for two years and was consumed by thoughts of killing himself, which he ultimately did some time later.

Andrés concluded that love was far more dangerous than any mountain.

Andrés remembered a moment from the first vacation he took with his father after his mother's death. He was eighteen and into all kinds of drugs. They were seated on the terrace of a hotel in Bariloche that looked out on Lake Nahuel Huapi. They drank champagne from six in the evening until the summer sun finally set in the southern sky. They exchanged opinions on the advantages and disadvantages of whisky compared to marijuana. Andrés didn't bring up the topic of drugs as a way to challenge his paternal authority (although he may have preferred that his father be alarmed or even a little angry with him). He merely wished to alleviate his father's pain, which is why he recommended his favorite anesthetic. He just wanted his father to forget about his dead wife for a while.

He was shocked in Plaza de Mulas by the amount of garbage that had accumulated in the area surrounding the Red Cross tents: gas canisters, metallic candy wrappers, tin cans. Andrés wasn't so bothered by the garbage itself as much as he was by the crowds of people it meant were there, especially since he would have to stay in Plaza de Mulas for several days. It would be necessary to ascend to Plaza Canadá, at 4,900 meters, to set up a cache of supplies and food and return to Plaza de Mulas remaining there until he was completely acclimatized. It was bitterly cold. His breath formed ice crystals and it took three hours to heat a liter of water. The effects of the high altitude—they were at 4,200 meters—were beginning to be felt. People tired more quickly and some became short of breath just from walking. To top it all, snow began to fall on the second day.

An Englishwoman who was much younger than Andrés tried to seduce him. Refusing her advances was simple. During the ascent the majority of climbers forgot about sex, perhaps due to the fact that no one bathed or changed their underwear for the entire period. Swollen, dehydrated lips and chaffed skin, in spite of the sunscreen, also helped to quash desire. Andrés had never had a girlfriend nor—as far as he knew—accidental children. In Buenos Aires he usually frequented prostitutes and his refusal to get involved meant that he never slept with the same one twice. Notwithstanding, he enjoyed sitting at a sidewalk café watching women stroll by. When one attracted him he would follow her. He was drawn to human stories and considered himself to be a kind of tourist in others' lives. Protected by this role as professional tourist, Andrés felt immune to rejection. He approached women completely uninhibited. In spite of his isolation he knew how to simulate existing social codes, much like an anthropologist who speaks the native language well enough to get by and understands customs and rituals. However, he was never entirely able to prevent his observational coldness from shining through. Women quickly realized what they were in for and would dump him, but it didn't much bother him since his primary objective was simply to shoot the breeze. He quickly grew bored with them. Finding common denominators in all their stories called into question the belief that people are in fact very different from one another: the myth of infinite human variability. The same happened to him when it

came to landscapes. For instance, all the lakes in southern Argentina looked the same to him: more or less the
same pine trees and rocks, some lakes were more green,
others more blue, steep mountain slopes, with or without
snow. He dissected nature with his gaze, putting it to a
kind of chemical analysis that reduced it to its component
parts. It was the movement of his body through the natural landscape that appealed to him. He found pleasure
in forcing himself to test the limits of his resistance. He
often wondered why at forty years of age he kept enduring
the nuisances of mountain climbing, but he realized that
nothing else afforded him the happiness that the mountains did. He loved stuffing his pockets with trail mix
so that while he climbed he could stick his hands into
the dark recesses of his clothing and retrieve handfuls of
almonds, raisins, chocolate, and lint to snack on.

On the fourth day of acclimatization he decided to set
off for Plaza de Mulas. Impatience had pushed him to
the edge of losing self-control. Every night up until then
he had snorted three lines of cocaine traced out on the
lid of an army-issue mess kit. He never did more than
three lines per day, not because he had to ration it (he had
brought a big enough stash to last several months), rather
he believed in the practice of self-discipline. He resolved
to depart before tedium caused him to cross the line.

It was a 1,400-meter climb between Plaza de Mulas
and Nido de Cóndores. Andrés stopped at Plaza Canadá
to gather up the supplies and food he'd stored there and
continued upward without stopping. Although he had
brought a high altitude tent with him, at Nido de Cóndores the wind forced him to spend the night together

with several other climbers in the rescue patrol's tent, which was reinforced with steel supports and heavy cables. Andrés remembered that on one of his first ascents the rescue patrol's tent was uprooted by the wind and he had been awoken suddenly to find himself exposed to the elements and gazing up at the star-filled sky. His tent mates offered him abundant broth and hot tea, which was greatly appreciated in a place where water was obtained through the laborious procedure of melting snow. In spite of the hospitality and the ferocious howling of the wind Andrés left at dawn for Refugio Berlín where he hoped to camp alone.

Being at such a high altitude and looking down from the top of the world, above the clouds and surrounding mountains fascinated Andrés. Though it seemed strange to him that right where you were closest to the sky there was less oxygen; that where the air was most pure there was less of it. He had climbed in the Himalayas twice without oxygen. His survival instinct would click in and warn him of the danger of dying from asphyxiation. On those occasions he feared having climbed to the point of no return, like a deep-sea diver suffering from apnea who sinks to such a depth that he doesn't know if he has enough air left to return to the surface. The conditions now were not as drastic. Refugio Berlín was only at an altitude of 6,000 meters. It would be harder to think clearly, he would get short of breath from the slightest effort, but he liked the idea of taking advantage of the lack of oxygen to feel lightheaded and goofy like when he smoked marijuana. He didn't have any marijuana with him now but he could do all the cocaine he wanted. Surrounded by climbers in Nido de Cóndores he had been unable to do so. He exited the tent on several occasions with the excuse of needing to urinate but the wind had thwarted both plans. Alone in his one-man tent that night in Refugio Berlín Andrés recalled tales of junkie climbers: mountaineering drug addicts who would shoot up while climbing until they overdosed. It was the kind of story that circulated among climbers in Nepal.

He awoke at sunrise thinking it would be a perfect day to reach the summit. The temperature was only a few degrees below zero with light winds and scattered clouds. He would have to cross La Canaleta, an expansive talus field of loose rock that would give way underfoot triggering small landslides and causing exasperating delays. Many climbers would give up when faced with this obstacle even though they were only a few hundred meters from the top. As he hiked slowly and deliberately, testing the stability of each rock and clinging to the right wall of La Canaleta, Andrés pondered his decision to remain on the summit. In 1988 a Spaniard had stayed up there for 67 days, and by the time he finally came down he had lost 15 kilos in body weight. It was a fearsome place. Climbers habitually made the summit, took photos next to the Cruz de la Cumbre, jotted a quick message in the Libro de Cumbre and hastily descended, afraid that a snowstorm would be unleashed upon them with 100 kilometer-per-hour winds sweeping them into the air like feathers and dropping them into a frozen abyss.

Andrés had resolved to never come down; he would remain at the summit. The idea had tempted him for a number of years. He repeatedly told himself that he had lived long enough. The place where the earth touched the sky seemed like the most appropriate to attempt an escape from the confinement of life (even though the paradoxical rules of life made escape impossible, since it could only be achieved by ceasing to exist). He would disappear into an abyss as if he had never existed. He would relinquish his fate to the arbitrary mountain winds. He would allow himself the temptation of surrendering to the cold and the desire to slip into a deep sleep. He was seduced by the vision of his body being buried and incorruptibly preserved in everlasting snows. Perhaps he would wander lost in the wind until he let himself plummet off of some precipice along the Pared Sur.

Translated by Darrell B. Lockhart

The South

Jorge Luis Borges

THE MAN WHO LANDED in Buenos Aires in 1871 bore the name of Johannes Dahlmann and he was a minister in the Evangelical Church. In 1939, one of his grandchildren, Juan Dahlmann, was secretary of a municipal library on Calle Córdoba, and he considered himself profoundly Argentinian. His maternal grandfather had been that Francisco Flores, of the Second Line-Infantry Division, who had died on the frontier of Buenos Aires, run through with a lance by Indians from Catriel; in the

JORGE LUIS BORGES (1899–1986) Internationally known for his many collections of short fiction, essays, and poems, Borges is by far Argentina's most celebrated writer. As a reader and translator of world literature himself and former director of the National Library, his contributions to the literary world are vast and incomparable. While he is perhaps best known for his innovative narrative style, his writings often encompass national themes and are replete with local color and landscapes. "The South" ("El sur"), originally published in his collection *Ficciones* (1935-44), is probably one of his most anthologized stories.

discord inherent between his two lines of descent, Juan Dahlmann (perhaps driven to it by his Germanic blood) chose the line represented by his romantic ancestor, his ancestor of the romantic death. An old sword, a leather frame containing the daguerreotype of a blank-faced man with a beard, the dash and grace of certain music, the familiar strophes of *Martín Fierro,* the passing years, boredom and solitude, all went to foster this voluntary, but never ostentatious nationalism. At the cost of numerous small privations, Dahlmann had managed to save the empty shell of a ranch in the South which had belonged to the Flores family; he continually recalled the image of the balsamic eucalyptus trees and the great rose-colored house which had once been crimson. His duties, perhaps even indolence, kept him in the city. Summer after summer he contented himself with the abstract idea of possession and with the certitude that his ranch was waiting for him on a precise site in the middle of the plain. Late in February, 1939, something happened to him.

Blind to all fault, destiny can be ruthless at one's slightest distraction. Dahlmann had succeeded in acquiring, on that very afternoon, an imperfect copy of Weil's edition of *The Thousand and One Nights.* Eager to examine this find, he did not wait for the elevator but hurried up the stairs. In the obscurity, something brushed by his forehead: a bat, a bird? On the face of the woman who opened the door to him he saw horror engraved, and the hand he wiped across his face came away red with blood. The edge of a recently painted door which someone had forgotten to close had caused this wound. Dahlmann was able to fall asleep, but from the moment he awoke at dawn the

savor of all things was atrociously poignant. Fever wasted
him and the pictures in *The Thousand and One Nights*
served to illustrate nightmares. Friends and relatives paid
him visits and, with exaggerated smiles, assured him that
they thought he looked fine. Dahlmann listened to them
with a kind of feeble stupor and he marveled at their not
knowing that he was in hell. A week, eight days passed,
and they were like eight centuries. One afternoon, the
usual doctor appeared, accompanied by a new doctor, and
they carried him off to a sanitarium on the Calle Ecuador, for it was necessary to X-ray him. Dahlmann, in the
hackney coach which bore them away, thought that he
would, at last, be able to sleep in a room different from
his own. He felt happy and communicative. When he
arrived at his destination, they undressed him, shaved
his head, bound him with metal fastenings to a stretcher;
they shone bright lights on him until he was blind and
dizzy, auscultated him, and a masked man stuck a needle
into his arm. He awoke with a feeling of nausea, covered
with a bandage, in a cell with something of a well about
it; in the days and nights which followed the operation he
came to realize that he had merely been, up until then, in
a suburb of hell. Ice in his mouth did not leave the least
trace of freshness. During these days Dahlmann hated
himself in minute detail: he hated his identity, his bodily
necessities, his humiliation, the beard which bristled
upon his face. He stoically endured the curative measures,
which were painful, but when the surgeon told him he
had been on the point of death from septicemia, Dahlmann dissolved in tears of self-pity for his fate. Physical
wretchedness and the incessant anticipation of horrible

nights had not allowed him time to think of anything so abstract as death. On another day, the surgeon told him he was healing and that, very soon, he would be able to go to his ranch for convalescence. Incredibly enough, the promised day arrived.

Reality favors symmetries and slight anachronisms: Dahlmann had arrived at the sanitarium in a hackney coach and now a hackney coach was to take him to the Constitución station. The first fresh tang of autumn, after the summer's oppressiveness, seemed like a symbol in nature of his rescue and release from fever and death. The city, at seven in the morning, had not lost that air of an old house lent it by the night; the streets seemed like long vestibules, the plazas were like patios. Dahlmann recognized the city with joy on the edge of vertigo: a second before his eyes registered the phenomena themselves, he recalled the corners, the billboards, the modest variety of Buenos Aires. In the yellow light of the new day, all things returned to him.

Every Argentine knows that the South begins at the other side of Rivadavia. Dahlmann was in the habit of saying that this was no mere convention, that whoever crosses this street enters a more ancient and sterner world. From inside the carriage he sought out, among the new buildings, the iron grill window, the brass knocker, the arched door, the entrance way, the intimate patio.

At the railroad station he noted that he still had thirty minutes. He quickly recalled that in a café on the Calle Brazil (a few dozen feet from Yrigoyen's house) there was an enormous cat which allowed itself to be caressed as if it were a disdainful divinity. He entered the café. There was the cat, asleep. He ordered a cup of coffee, slowly stirred the sugar, sipped it (this pleasure had been denied him in the clinic), and thought, as he smoothed the cat's black coat, that this contact was an illusion and that the two beings, man and cat, were as good as separated by a glass, for man lives in time, in succession, while the magical animal lives in the present, in the eternity of the instant.

Along the next to the last platform the train lay waiting. Dahlmann walked through the coaches until he found one almost empty. He arranged his baggage in the network rack. When the train started off, he took down his valise and extracted, after some hesitation, the first volume of *The Thousand and One Nights*. To travel with this book, which was so much a part of the history of his ill fortune, was a kind of affirmation that his ill fortune had been annulled; it was a joyous and secret defiance of the frustrated forces of evil.

Along both sides of the train the city dissipated into suburbs; this sight, and then a view of the gardens and villas, delayed the beginning of his reading. The truth was that Dahlmann read very little. The magnetized mountain and the genie who swore to kill his benefactor are—who would deny it?—marvelous, but not so much more than the morning itself and the mere fact of being. The joy of life distracted him from paying attention to Scheherezade and her superfluous miracles. Dahlmann closed his book and allowed himself to live.

Lunch—the bouillon served in shining metal bowls, as in the remote summers of childhood—was one more peaceful and rewarding delight.

Tomorrow I'll wake up at the ranch, he thought, and it

was as if he were two men at a time: the man who traveled through the autumn day and across the geography of the fatherland, and the other one, locked up in a sanitarium and subject to methodical servitude. He saw unplastered brick houses, long and angled, timelessly watching the trains go by; he saw horsemen along the dirt roads; he saw gullies and lagoons and ranches; he saw great luminous clouds that resembled marble; and all these things were accidental, casual, like dreams of the plain. He also thought he recognized trees and crop fields; but he would not have been able to name them, for his actual knowledge of the countryside was quite inferior to his nostalgic and literary knowledge.

From time to time he slept, and his dreams were animated by the impetus of the train. The intolerable white sun of high noon had already become the yellow sun which precedes nightfall, and it would not be long before it would turn red. The railroad car was now also different; it was not the same as the one which had quit the station siding at Constitución; the plain and the hours had transfigured it. Outside, the moving shadow of the railroad car stretched toward the horizon. The elemental earth was not perturbed either by settlements or other signs of humanity. The country was vast but at the same time intimate and, in some measure, secret. The limitless country sometimes contained only a solitary bull. The solitude was perfect, perhaps hostile, and it might have occurred to Dahlmann that he was traveling into the past and not merely south. He was distracted from these considerations by the railroad inspector who, on reading his ticket, advised him that the train would not let him off at the regular station but at another: an earlier stop, one scarcely known to Dahlmann. (The man added an explanation which Dahlmann did not attempt to understand, and which he hardly heard, for the mechanism of events did not concern him.)

The train laboriously ground to a halt, practically in the middle of the plain. The station lay on the other side of the tracks; it was not much more than a siding and a shed. There was no means of conveyance to be seen, but the station chief supposed that the traveler might secure a vehicle from a general store and inn to be found some ten or twelve blocks away.

Dahlmann accepted the walk as a small adventure. The sun had already disappeared from view, but a final splendor exalted the vivid and silent plain, before the night erased its color. Less to avoid fatigue than to draw out his enjoyment of these sights, Dahlmann walked slowly, breathing in the odor of clover with sumptuous joy.

The general store at one time had been painted a deep scarlet, but the years had tempered this violent color for its own good. Something in its poor architecture recalled a steel engraving, perhaps one from an old edition of *Paul et Virginie*. A number of horses were hitched up to the paling. Once inside, Dahlmann thought he recognized the shopkeeper. Then he realized that he had been deceived by the man's resemblance to one of the male nurses in the sanitarium. When the shopkeeper heard Dahlmann's request, he said he would have the shay made up. In order to add one more event to that day and to kill time, Dahlmann decided to eat at the general store.

Some country louts, to whom Dahlmann did not at first

pay any attention, were eating and drinking at one of the tables. On the floor, and hanging on to the bar, squatted an old man, immobile as an object. His years had reduced and polished him as water does a stone or the generations of men do a sentence. He was dark, dried up, diminutive, and seemed outside time, situated in eternity. Dahlmann noted with satisfaction the kerchief, the thick poncho, the long *chiripá*, and the colt boots, and told himself, as he recalled futile discussions with people from the Northern counties or from the province of Entre Rios, that gauchos like this no longer existed outside the South.

Dahlmann sat down next to the window. The darkness began overcoming the plain, but the odor and sound of the earth penetrated the iron bars of the window. The shop owner brought him sardines, followed by some roast meat. Dahlmann washed the meal down with several glasses of red wine. Idling, he relished the tart savor of the wine, and let his gaze, now grown somewhat drowsy, wander over the shop. A kerosene lamp hung from a beam. There were three customers at the other table: two of them appeared to be farm workers; the third man, whose features hinted at Chinese blood, was drinking with his hat on. All of a sudden, Dahlmann felt something brush lightly against his face. Next to the heavy glass of turbid wine, upon one of the stripes in the table cloth, lay a spit ball of breadcrumb. That was all: but someone had thrown it there.

The men at the other table seemed totally cut off from him. Perplexed, Dahlmann decided that nothing had happened, and he opened the volume of *The Thousand and One Nights,* by way of suppressing reality. After a few

moments another little ball landed on his table, and now
the *peones* laughed outright. Dahlmann said to himself
that he was not frightened, but he reasoned that it would
be a major blunder if he, a convalescent, were to allow
himself to be dragged by strangers into some chaotic
quarrel. He determined to leave, and had already gotten
to his feet when the owner came up and exhorted him in
an alarmed voice:

"*Señor* Dahlmann, don't pay any attention to those
lads; they're half crocked."

Dahlmann was not surprised to learn that the other
man, now, knew his name. But he felt that these concilia-
tory words served only to aggravate the situation. Previous to this moment, the *peones*' provocation was directed
against an unknown face, against no one in particular,
almost against no one at all. Now it was an attack against
him, against his name, and his neighbors knew it. Dahlmann pushed the owner aside, confronted the *peones*, and
demanded to know what they wanted of him.

The tough guy with a Chinese look staggered heavily
to his feet. Almost in Juan Dahlmann's face he shouted
insults, as if he had been a long way off. His game was to
exaggerate his drunkenness, and this extravagance consti-
tuted a ferocious mockery. Between curses and obsceni-
ties, he threw a long knife into the air, followed it with
his eyes, caught and juggled it, and challenged Dahlmann
to a knife fight. The owner objected in a tremulous voice,
pointing out that Dahlmann was unarmed. At this point,
something unforeseeable occurred.

From a corner of the room, the old motionless gaucho—in whom Dahlmann saw a summary and cipher of

the South (his South)—threw him a naked dagger, which landed at his feet. It was as if the South had resolved that Dahlmann should accept the duel. Dahlmann bent over to pick up the dagger, and felt two things. The first, that this almost instinctive act bound him to fight. The second, that the weapon, in his torpid hand, was no defense at all, but would merely serve to justify his murder. He had once played with a poniard, like all men, but his idea of fencing and knife-play did not go further than the notion that all strokes should be directed upwards, with the cutting edge held inwards. *They would not have allowed such things to happen to me in the sanitarium,* he thought.

"Let's get on our way," said the other man.

They went out and if Dahlmann was without hope, he was also without fear. As he crossed the threshold, he felt that to die in a knife fight, under the open sky, and going forward to the attack, would have been a liberation, a joy, and a festive occasion, on the first night in the sanitarium, when they stuck him with the needle. He felt that if he had been able to choose, then, or to dream his death, this would have been the death he would have chosen or dreamt.

Firmly clutching his knife, which he perhaps would not know how to wield, Dahlmann went out into the plain.

Translated by Anthony Kerrigan

Arrowheads

Luisa Peluffo

> Reality favors symmetries and slight
> anachronisms.
>
> —Jorge Luis Borges, "The South"

AT TWENTY SHE TRAVELED to Europe and there,
she discovered the past. In each and every city where she
traveled there were traces and imprints of primitive settlements. In Rome, as she walked by the Forum, she would
brush her fingers across the ancient stones. In Sevilla,
she saw the foundation of Greek temples under Mudejar
walls, in Barcelona the Gothic Quarter and in Paris, the
Roman ruins at Arènes de Lutèce.

LUISA PELUFFO (1941–) A resident of San Carlos de
Bariloche in the province of Rio Negro, Patagonia, since 1977,
Peluffo still maintains strong literary ties with her native Buenos Aires. Keenly aware that for some, moving to Bariloche
means "te caes del mapa," ("you fall off the map"), she authored
an instruction manual titled *Me voy a vivir al sur* on how to
emigrate south to the Patagonia. Her most recent novel, *Nadie
baila el tango* (2008), was awarded the Premio Unico from the
city of Buenos Aires.

When she returned to Buenos Aires, her desire to explore the past did not wane but everything just seemed too recent.

"There's no past here," she'd say.

One day she read a tourist brochure advertising weekend trips. One of them suggested: *Visit the land of the Coliqueo, Los Toldos, and the Salamanca Lagoon.*

"Come on, let's go," she said to her boyfriend. "It says here Los Toldos is so named because of the Indian huts."

"There aren't any Indians, they all died back in the 1870s in the Conquest of the Desert."

"Why did they have to be killed . . . ? Couldn't they have been civilized?"

"In the United States they did the exact same thing."

"Wow, just look at the example you gave me . . . It doesn't matter, I still want to go, I'm curious; one of Coliqueo's descendants might still be alive."

Her boyfriend liked the idea of a weekend in Los Toldos, but couldn't have cared less about the Indians.

"The Coliqueo were Mapuche, which means 'Earth people.' Did you know that?" she remarked after looking it up in the encyclopedia.

"No."

"*Mapu* is earth and *che* is people, and do you know what Coliqueo means?"

"I haven't a clue."

"Dark Flint."

"Really? You don't say!"

"'. . . Ignacio Coliqueo,'" she continued reading from the encyclopedia, "'born in Boroa (Chile), died in 1871 in the Province of Buenos Aires, was a famous chief and colonel in the Argentine Army who enlisted, along with his tribe, in the army of General Urquiza. After lending a helping hand to overthrow Rosas, the Coliqueo established a town, which was later destroyed by other tribes like them, but followers of Rosas, on the site that thereafter would be called Los Toldos.' Isn't that incredible?"

"Uh-huh."

And so they took off in their recently purchased secondhand Citroën.

"I'm taking this little suitcase," she announced pulling a suitcase of the type you would take on an expedition to the Ranquel Indians.

"If I don't take a suitcase, it's like I'm not traveling," she added while shoving it into the back seat.

But in Los Toldos there wasn't a single indication that the Coliqueo had ever set foot there. There wasn't even a hotel, only a brick house on a corner, indicating "Lodging." So they continued on to Junín. Similarly there were no vestiges of huts or Indian villages. At last, they found a boarding house. The double bed, covered with a red sateen bedspread, almost completely filled the room and all they could see of the carpet was some brown with ornate yellow designs. But she was able to open and close her suitcase and slept hoping that nearby, somewhere, there would be a trace of the Coliqueo.

They returned the next day to Los Toldos, stopping first at a gas station. A large burly dark-skinned man, stood next to the pump.

"Ask him," she said.

He got out of the car, said fill-it-up, and checked the

tires but never did ask anything. While the man filled the tank, she pushed opened the wing window and asked:

"Do you know where the land of the Coliqueo is?"

"What?"

"The land of the Coliqueo," she repeated and showed him the brochure.

"I'm Coliqueo," he answered unexpectedly, touching his chest.

"Dark Flint," she muttered.

"Come again?" he asked.

"No, nothing," she responded. And tried to imagine him on a horse with a spear but couldn't. Instead, she remembered the time when she'd gone to a restaurant in the Abasto, a shopping mall that was once the central wholesale fruit and vegetable market of the city. Several folkloric groups were performing that day. Standing guard on either side of a platform—where some alleged gauchos tapped out a *malambo* with their boots—were two men just like this one. They were bare-chested with long dark shoulder-length hair held back in a hair band, and they stood looking savagely straight ahead. Each man grasped a spear with a stone arrowhead tied to its tip. She also recalled that to get to the bathroom, she had to skirt around the platform forcing her to pass right by them, close enough to notice that one of them had a flesh colored band-aid on his muscular arm that was holding the spear.

"The one that made this place famous was Evita. Did you know she was born here?" said the Coliqueo, interrupting her memory. The noise of the gas pump stopped.

"Yeah?"

"Yeah, in La Unión, don Duarte's ranch," he squatted to tighten the gas tank cap. "My family used to work that land."

"Oh"

"There's a lot of Coliqueo around here," he informed her, wiping his hands on a dirty rag. "Want me to clean the windshield?"

Afterwards, she and her boyfriend continued on to the Salamanca Lagoon, which was no different than any other lagoon in Buenos Aires province. They spent the afternoon at a convent of Benedictine monks where they bought freshly made cheese and homemade jam and visited a small chapel, the oldest thing they found.

Within the year they got married and spent their honeymoon in the south. They camped out in a place called Valle Encantado, on the banks of the Limay River, and when she went to drive in one of the tent stakes, she found an arrowhead. There was the past. She decided to keep it as a good luck charm.

That first night, the murmur of the sparkling waters in the darkness made them feel as if they were part of the great mystery. They defied sleep. At dawn, they remained in rapture, as a surreal mist slowly hovered over the water.

Legend asserts, he said the day before they broke camp, if you bathe in the Limay you will return here. Then, guarded by the wind-sculpted figures on the massive rock walls, they sat on the bank, took off their shoes, and dipped their feet into the transparent water.

Reluctantly they returned to Buenos Aries and shortly thereafter they had a son: Nahuel. After that they returned to the south, this time to live. He built a cabin on Lake Gutiérrez and she wrote a book and planted two birch trees. And they had another son: Pehuén.

Each year in mid-December they drove across the deserted plains to spend the holidays with the rest of their family. On one of these return trips in the sweltering heat without air conditioning they stopped near Piedra del Aguila, a small village. They parked their car under some trees next to a pasture where several horses calmly grazed. They wanted to rest awhile, eat something, and, above all else, let the kids out after being cooped up so long in the car.

Nahuel, drowsy from the heat and the long hours of traveling, asked if they were far from Bariloche. Pehuén woke up and began to cry.

She searched for her bag in the back seat, hauled it out, opened it, and pulled out the baby bottle with water. Besides water, she carried a little bit of everything in that bag: sandwiches, crackers, a towel, cologne, toilet paper, and even her jewelry box, just in case thieves broke into the cabin while they were away.

They stretched their legs, ate, and when they were putting their belongings back into the car, they saw Pehuén running excitedly toward the horses. They both took off running after him and caught him just as he was about to run headlong into a dappled gray horse. They returned to the car and continued on their journey.

When they arrived at Valle Encantado, the halfway point between Piedra del Aguila and Bariloche, she looked for her bag in the backseat. It wasn't there. There wasn't any bag there. Even today when she thinks about it, she still has a sinking feeling in the pit of her stomach. She shouted, "It's not here!" Her husband told her to look in the trunk, stopping the car on the shoulder. "I didn't put it in the trunk," she answered. And, there was another stab to her heart. "I didn't put it anywhere," she repeated, "it's back in Piedra del Aguila." Just the same she ran to look in the trunk. "No, it's not there. We must have left it next to the car when we went running after Pehuén. Let's go back."

He puts the car in gear and turns back toward Piedra del Aguila. Nahuel asks: "Are we there yet?" Pehuén, his damp cheek against her chest, remained asleep.

Although she is hopeful, she doesn't want to think about it. But she recalls: her watch, her Aunt Emma's pearl necklace, her grandmother's choker, the medal from her first communion, her mother's brooch, and her gold ring. Also, the arrowhead she'd found during their first trip, along the banks of the Limay.

They arrive back at the spot, their tire tracks still visible, but not a hint of the bag. There are a few ranches nearby. They walk toward them, clap their hands, and the dogs bark. Some boys peer out, their faces all wind-burned and streaked with dirt and snot. Children who are brought up in the Patagonia always have dirt and snot on their faces, she thinks, hers too. They ask. Nobody knows anything.

It's almost dark when they get back on the road. Now the Patagonia looks gray and hostile. Her husband asks what was in the bag. She still hadn't told him about the jewelry box. So she does and he asks what was in the box. As they leave the Valle Encantado behind, she weeps in silence.

Back in Bariloche her uneasiness grows, as if the cord that tied her to her small familiar world had abruptly been severed. Sometimes, still, the sorrow returns.

He doesn't understand. They're just things, he'd say, trying to console her, nothing more than things . . .

They grow apart. And she knows then that she's lost him. He doesn't stay in the south. She does. And there she raises her sons, and teaches classes in two schools, and stacks wood, and stands in line in the snow to get kerosene, and curses the cold, the rain, the ice and the damn car that won't start.

Years later—her sons now grown men—on one of her endless trips across the Patagonian desert heading toward Madryn, she sees a sign along the side of the road:

TOMB OF CHIEF INACAYAL

She backs up and guides the car over a trail that leads to the base of a small hill. There, in the middle of the earthy vastness, was the monument. She gets out of the car and climbs up the slope. At the top, she finds a precarious structure in extremely poor condition, abandoned, and in ruins.

She gets back on the road. Inacayal . . . she doesn't know what the chief's name means and while traveling along she remembers Dark Flint and when she'd gone in search of the land of the Coliqueo.

At Paso de Indios, she stops to get gas. Like Piedra del Aguila and the majority of small Patagonian villages, Paso de Indios is divided by the highway with a few run-down houses grouped together on either side.

There at the service station, next to the pumps, an

old woman and boy offer up something in a box, something to sell to the tourists. She goes over to them. The old woman—motionless and indifferent—holds a sign saying:

MAPUCHE ARROWHEADS. 4 PESOS.

"Grandma makes 'em to use as pendants," says the boy and he shakes the pile of arrowheads that are in the box until he picks one out.

"For you," he says, with a smile.

Translated by Beth Pollack

The Desert

Cristina Siscar

THE HORIZON, like a whiff of smoke, had begun to dissolve shortly after noon. As the bus advanced southward, farther and farther south, the dusty brown plains and the overcast skies merged into a drab gray. And straight ahead, a ribbon of asphalt, scarcely one stretch of the route that went all the way to the Straits of Magellan, a stretch that despite the distance always appeared the same.

In the course of the afternoon, they had only encoun-

CRISTINA SISCAR (1947–) Although born in Buenos Aires, Siscar lived in exile in Paris from 1980 through 1986, where she began her literary career. Since returning to Argentina, she has published two collections of her own stories and edited four anthologies of short fiction. She has been awarded a number of important literary prizes from the National Foundation for the Arts and the Konex Foundation for her forays into fantastic literature. Her story "Bastidores, hilo y cañamazo" was recognized by the Permament Assembly on Human Rights of Argentina and was published in translation as "Hoop, Thread, and Canvas" in Gwendolyn Díaz's *Women and Power in Argentine Literature* (2007).

tered one other long-distance bus that was traveling the other way; once, a car going at full speed had passed them by; later on, they spotted a refrigerator truck. Then came a period of lethargy that seemed endless. At one point, a flock of rheas had collected in the middle of the highway, blocking it and not caring that they were being honked at, not even the slightest escape reflex: the creatures kept just knocking into each other like they were dazed or hypnotized by the presence of something so mobile. But no sooner were they left behind than their drab gray plumage vanished into the gray and barren landscape, unbroken even by a wire fence.

And suddenly night fell, just like that, a black curtain. A uniform and total blackness. Not so much as a hint of a reflection in the windows, not even the dark shadow of a tree, not even a star. Nothing else, up ahead, just the glare of the bus's headlights, which was hidden by the high backs of the seats.

Then they put on a movie. Since the TV screen was far off, Mutis couldn't hear the voices, and he couldn't really make out the Spanish subtitles, either. The colors flickered—images of skyscrapers and big city streets, must have been New York—floated in the semi-darkness.

Mutis got the feeling that the whole bus was floating, that they had left the Earth down below. Perhaps hypnotized, too, just like the rheas, by the fleeting images from the TV, he fell asleep. When he opened his eyes, the screen was black. It was like going from one dream to another. A bucking motion shook him. The bus had pulled off the road and was braking; the lights came on and the low-pitched voice of the driver announced that they were stopping for forty-five minutes.

In the light of the yellow bulbs, sunken into the night, the rest stop looked like a prefabricated concrete box that could have been set up just yesterday only to be taken down tomorrow, without leaving a trace. Two trucks and a tour bus were lined up on the esplanade out front. Mutis walked through whirlwinds of dust; the freezing wind cut right through his clothes and skin. He had been the last to get off; the other passengers, not more than ten or twelve, had already gone inside the building.

Inside, everything was discolored from the white light of the fluorescent tubes. To the right there was a big room where a waiter was coming and going in between the formica tables, most of them empty, even though this was where almost all the travelers would eventually end up hanging out. It seemed like an excessive space, useless, designed to comfortably accommodate the multitudes that had never arrived. On a high shelf in one corner a TV was showing scenes from an accident that had just occurred on another road, one with more traffic, in some far-off distant part of the country. Mute scenes. Because the music broadcast by the speakers made it impossible to hear anything else. It was one of those repetitive songs with a tropical rhythm that you danced to in place, one step forward, one step back.

Mutis meandered through the various successive areas of the place, which had no partitions to separate them, like the different neighborhoods of a city. In one corner, on the other side of the restaurant, they were selling lottery tickets and assorted scratch card games, and there was a stand with an endless succession of knickknacks, all mixed up and all covered in dust. Then there were the video games, where a kid was pressing buttons in front of a screen on which an automobile was zigzagging to get around obstacles, through cities, meadows, and mountains, in splendid colors. Next there was a place to have a drink: a long bar with tall stools and then a couple of tables in between artificial plants; farther back, forgotten, a foosball table and a pool table; and still farther, at the very end, a completely empty space reminiscent of a dance floor. Maybe because of the music, which even there was deafening.

Though he didn't really feel like having anything, Mutis went up to the bar. Two backpackers were poring over a map that they had spread out over one of the tables, completely absorbed by it, like they were searching amongst the dots and dashes on that paper for whatever it was that the unchanging landscape had been keeping from them. At another table, a woman and two men— all three very blond, very freckled—were drinking beer. Mutis ordered a coffee.

The girl that took his order smiled at him when she did so, and she smiled at him again when she deposited the little cup and saucer. There was nothing strange in a waiter or a waitress giving a customer a routine, professional smile, like a kind of tic. But there was something in that smile that caught his attention: it was so cold. Out of inertia, he turned around to watch while the girl waited on a truck driver with deep circles under his eyes who didn't so much as even glance up at her. Again and again the smile had been repeated, identical: head rigid, thin lips that just barely opened, not one millimeter more or less, exactly the same duration. Switched on, switched off. It was like watching someone exercise her muscles in front of a mirror, except that that someone was blind.

After the coffee, Mutis ordered a grappa, scrutinizing the smile now. Click. It was really a grimace projected for an instant onto a face of wax. Perhaps that was what it was: the waxen face, the high cheekbones, the almond-shaped eyes, the dark, straight hair. The waitress remained in front of him, impassive, like she was looking at him without seeing him. Mutis thought that because of the din of the music she might not have heard him, and he said again, "Grappa," making the usual sign with his fingers to indicate the measure of a shot glass. It seemed like she was trying to read his lips. Right away, without batting an eye, the girl spun around on her heels and headed for the very end of the bar, stopping in front of the cashier. He took a bottle down off of a shelf and handed it to her. Then she brought the glass, grimace, click.

A little intoxicated already, raising their glasses in a toast, the blond guys and the woman laughed heartily around the table (this could only be deduced by way of their contortions, because the speakers were still pounding out the same rhythm). You could easily make out the blood of the old settlers to the region when you looked at these people. Although you could also tell— by the expensive coats designed for European snows, the detached demeanor of the tourist, the indifference—the fact that they, unlike their ancestors, would do little more than take a quick look around and then keep on going.

The waitress, in the meantime, was coming and going, working the espresso machine, waiting on people, washing cups. Always rigid; it was like her eyes were looking for something inside her head that was either very far away or very high up, and the intermittent projection on her face: an Oriental automaton. Who knew where she was from, thought Mutis, who was now curious. Probably, she was Vietnamese. Or Chinese. Or Korean. Stuck here, on the other side of the planet, in a wasteland. With all that incessant wind outside, surrounded by those desert plains, he could not get enough of the human landscape inside, in constant motion: all those hours of not seeing anything neither behind nor ahead, of not knowing where he was going, no longer mattered anymore.

She was constantly wiping down the bar, whose aluminum surface had lost its shine, never to get it back again. She was wiping it without giving the dust time to settle, without pause. When she was in front of him again, Mutis asked her where she was from. Since she didn't show any signs of having heard him and was already continuing on her rounds, he leaned in over the bar and said again, "Where? Where are you from?" raising his voice. Then she smiled instantaneously, went up to the cash register, and returned one minute later with his tab. She took his money, smile, bye.

At the table, the backpackers were sliding their fingers eagerly over the laminated map, demanding answers. If it had been made of cardboard, they would have torn the edges. The tour guide came to get them, also taking the beer-drinkers, who left behind a mountain of empty cans.

But the girl was still there, synchronized arms and legs, eyes fixed and blind. She had brought a sandwich to the truck driver, who was reading the paper; she was carrying cups, drying glasses, and then she started cleaning again, cloth in hand: trapped in that little strip between the wall and the bar. Mutis was waiting.

Someone tapped him on the shoulder: it was the driver, who pointed to his watch and then walked away, slowly. Mutis didn't move. She was coming back now, scrubbing with her cloth, fast, she was already passing him . . . But no, Mutis grabbed her arm, squeezed it. And very close to her face, where the smile was sketched and erased in rapid succession, he said, almost whispering, "What is your name?" There was no reply, just that fixed stare in her cold eyes. Then he shouted, "Your name!" They stayed like that for a few seconds—the echo of the words vibrating between them—until he let her go and she resumed her interrupted movements, moving away toward the opposite side of the bar, where a man in a woolen cap was dozing off.

And back through the video games. The kid in front of the screen was persisting in his race along eternal landscapes, completely engrossed in the image of a machine traveling around inside another machine. In the restaurant, there were three people left who seemed to be distractedly watching television. Suddenly, outside, he was caught off guard by the silence and the gusts of wind that rocked the darkness.

When the bus started up again, Mutis turned to face the building on the side of the road. He thought he could make out the waitress in one of the windows: the white oval of her face against the glass looked like it had been superimposed onto the reflection of the departing bus, in which Mutis was pressing his eyelashes against the bus window, his gaze fixed on that spot. Later on, the image appeared in his dreams; and upon waking, at dawn, everything, outside of the bus windows, had that same bone-white, blank color. His mind, too, was blank, as he sat there hunkered down in his seat. Another passenger informed him that he had to get off: they had arrived.

From the side of the highway, while he was waiting, struggling against the wind, for some vehicle to take him the rest of the way, Mutis could see the pale sea and, at sea level, the glare of the sun, still hazy in the fog. Some ways off the coast you could see a ship at anchor, fuzzy at first, slowly but surely clearer—kind of like a child's drawing done in pencil, a mere outline, indistinguishable from the sea—as the fog continued to dissipate.

Finally, a pick-up truck stopped. The driver explained to Mutis that he was going to be turning off two kilometers before Lihuén, but that he could always go on foot the rest of the way. They took a dirt road; it was a pretty rough ride. On one side and on the other, the same plains with the same dry, sparse grass, not so much as a shadow, except for a few dark birds that crossed the sky like arrows, headed north. After a few minutes, they made out two silhouettes coming up the road. They turned out to be two burly guys. Mutis was struck by the frizzy hair on their heads and the excess of reddish hair on their faces.

"Russians," said the driver, smiling.

Since Mutis looked at him uncomprehendingly, the man added, "You didn't see the ship in the gulf? It's a freighter with a Soviet flag on it. A ship from a state that's just been dissolved. Can you imagine? It's had to just stay there, stranded, in the hopes that someone will claim it, give it an identity. So for the past month or so, the sailors just drift around, on land, like vagrants, begging."

Mutis turned around. In the cloud of dust the truck had raised, the figures had disappeared. He suddenly remembered the girl with the almond-shaped eyes, saw her face in the glass, although a little steamed-up now, far away. He was about to say, "Last night, at the rest stop we stopped at . . ." But at that moment they stopped, too; they had reached the spot where the road forked.

"Can I ask," said the driver, "what you're going to Lihuén for?" and his face was solemn as he heard Mutis out.

There was a pause. The man gazed at the windshield, at the smudges of the insects that had been smashed, until finally he got up the courage to say—at that moment, in that place—that there was no point in going all the way there, that they had closed the mine and everyone had already left, that the place was deserted, in ruins. The door slamming cut him short: he was talking to himself. Mutis had already gotten out and was waving to him with his arm up high. Very quickly the truck veered off left, disappearing rapidly, into a dust devil.

Frozen, with that wind that went right through him and was beginning to cover him in dust, Mutis thought he would end up indistinguishable from the landscape. He was walking, but there was nothing to suggest he was making headway. On all sides the desert extended so far that it blended into the clouds, all enveloping, like an empty sphere.

Translated by Jennifer Croft

JILL GIBIAN is Professor of Spanish and Latin American Studies at Eastern Oregon University. As a Fulbright Scholar, she has been committed to studying and translating the literature and culture of the River Plate region of Argentina and Uruguay. She is particularly interested in the study of tango and in questions of memory and national identity as presented through literature and film of the Southern Cone. Her anthology, *Tango-Lit: Parodies of Passion* (forthcoming) focuses on the tango as cultural text.

RHONDA DAHL BUCHANAN is a Professor of Spanish and Director of Latin American and Latino Studies at the University of Louisville. She has published numerous critical studies on Latin American fiction and translations, including: *The Entre Ríos Trilogy* by Perla Suez, *Quick Fix: Sudden Fiction* by Ana María Shua, and *The Secret Gardens of Mogador* by Alberto Ruy-Sánchez (2006 NEA Literature Fellowship Project).

JENNIFER CROFT holds an MFA in Literary Translation from the University of Iowa and is currently completing a PhD in Comparative Literature at Northwestern University. Her translations have appeared in *Words With-*

out Borders, *World Literature Today*, and *Absinthe*, among others. She lives in Paris.

ALEXANDRA FALEK is Assistant Professor of Latin American literature and culture in the Department of Spanish and Portuguese at New York University. Her most recent translations have appeared in *Metamorphoses: A Journal of Literary Translation*. She is the current Managing Editor of the *Journal of Spanish Cultural Studies*.

MARINA HARSS currently works as a freelance writer and dance critic for the *New Yorker* and is a prolific translator from French, Spanish, and Italian. Her translations include Pier Paolo Pasolini's *Stories from the City of God* and *For Solo Violin* and Alberto Moravia's *Conjugal Love*. Her translations have appeared in *Words Without Borders, The Latin American Review, Flash Art International, Bomb,* and *Brooklyn Rail.* Her most recent translation is *Poem Strip* (NYRB Classics, 2009), a modern retelling of the Orpheus myth, by Dino Buzzati.

ANTHONY KERRIGAN (1918-1991) translated *Ficciones* and *A Personal Anthology* by Jorge Luis Borges, *Selected Poems* by Pablo Neruda, and Miguel de Unamuno's *Tragic Sense of Life in Men and Nations,* for which he won the National Book Award in 1973. In 1988, he was honored by the National Endowment for the Arts for his lifetime contributions to American letters.

ANDREA G. LABINGER is Professor of Spanish *Emerita* at the University of La Verne. Among the authors she has translated are Sabina Berman, Carlos Cerda, Mempo Giardinelli, Ana María Shua, and Luisa Valenzuela. *Call Me Magdalena*, Labinger's translation of Steimberg's *Cuando digo Magdalena* (University of Nebraska Press, 2001), was a finalist in the PEN International-California competition. *The Rainforest,* her translation of Steimberg's *La selva*, and *Casablanca and Other Stories* by Edgar Brau, the latter co-translated with Donald and Joanne Yates, were both finalists in the PEN-USA competition for 2007. Labinger's most recent translations are Daína Chaviano's *The Island of Eternal Love* (Riverhead/Penguin, 2008) and Angelina Muñiz-Huberman's *The Confidantes* (Gaon Books, 2009).

HELEN LANE (1921-2004) was an accomplished translator of Latin American fiction. Her long list of credits includes *Santa Evita* and *The Peron Novel* by Tomás Eloy Martínez; *A Fish in Water* by Mario Vargas Llosa; *Essays on Mexican Art* by Octavio Paz; *Massacre in Mexico* by Elena Poniatowska, and *Strange Things Happen Here* by Luisa Valenzuela, from which "A Place of Its Solitude" comes. At the time of her death, she was working on a six-volume autobiography of Victoria Ocampo together with Ronald Christ. She also translated literature from French, Italian, and Portuguese and worked in film subtitling.

SUZANNE JILL LEVINE is a distinguished translator of Latin America's most innovative writers.

Her many honors include PEN American and USA West awards, National Endowment for the Arts and National Endowment for the Humanities fellowships and grants and a Guggenheim Foundation Fellowship. Her books include *The Subversive Scribe: Translating Latin American Fiction* and *Manuel Puig and the Spider Woman: His Life and Fictions*. Most recently, she has edited five volumes of the works of Jorge Luis Borges for Penguin Classics.

DARRELL B. LOCKHART is an associate professor of Spanish at the University of Nevada, Reno, where he teaches Latin American literature, film, and popular culture. His research focuses primarily on Latin American Jewish literature and cultural production. He is the editor of *Jewish Writers of Latin America: A Dictionary* (1997), among other publications on this topic. In addition, he is the editor of the volumes *Latin American Science Fiction Writers: An A–Z Guide* (2004) and *Latin American Mystery Writers: An A–Z Guide* (2004). Aside from the authors included in this volume, Lockhart has translated the works of other Southern Cone authors including Silvia Plager, Manuela Fingueret, Elina Wechsler, and Emma Sepúlveda-Pulvirenti.

BETH POLLACK is Professor of Spanish and Director of Graduate Studies for the MA in Spanish at New Mexico State University. She researches contemporary Latin American fiction, particularly Latin American Jewish Fiction as well as translates literary texts from English to Spanish and Spanish to English. She has translated poetry and prose by Cuban, Cuban-American and U.S. authors (both into English and Spanish) as well as authors from Argentina and Bolivia which have been published in such venues as *Puerto del Sol*, *Puentelibre* and the ezine *Decir del* agua. She was a resident of the 2010 Banff International Literary Translation Centre.

GREGORY RABASSA has translated several major Latin American novelists from both Spanish and Portuguese, including Julio Cortázar, Jorge Amado, and Gabriel García Márquez. On the advice of Cortázar, García Márquez waited three years for Rabassa's schedule to become open so that he could translate *One Hundred Years of Solitude*. He later declared Rabassa's translation to be superior to his own Spanish original. Typically, Rabassa translates without reading the book beforehand, working as he goes. For his version of Cortázar's novel, *Hopscotch*, Rabassa received a National Book Award for Translation. Rabassa currently teaches at Queens College, where he is a Distinguished Professor. In 2006, he was awarded the National Medal of Arts. His book detailing his experiences as a translator, *If This Be Treason: Translation and Its Dyscontents, A Memoir*, was published by New Directions in 2006.

JOANNE M. YATES combines her interest in language and Latin American literature through the study of rhetoric and composition. Her earlier work in Latin American studies, particularly Argentine literature, prompted her to examine the process of translation. She has translated many conversations of Jorge Luis Borges, stories by Marco Denevi, and most currently the work of Edgar Brau, an author she admires for his intellectual integrity and philosophical insights.

Permissions

Permissions

Adolfo Bioy Casares, "About the Shape of the World," from *Selected Stories* (New York: New Directions) and translated by Suzanne Jill Levine. © 1978 Adolfo Bioy Casares; English © 1994 Suzanne Jill Levine. Reprinted by permission of the translator and New Directions Publishing Corp.

Marcelo Birmajer, "The Last Happy Family" originally published as "La última familia feliz" in *El fuego más alto* (Barcelona: Grupo Editorial Norma, 1997). Translated by Darrell B.Lockhart with permission of author.

Jorge Luis Borges, "The South" first published in the 1962 Grove Press English language edition of *Ficciones*, translated by Anthony Kerrigan. Reprinted by permission of Grove/Atlantic, Inc.

Edgar Brau, "The Blessing," from *Casablanca and other stories*, translated by Joanne M. Yates (East Lansing, MI: Michigan State University Press, 2006). Reprinted by permission of Michigan State University Press.

Carlos Chernov, "The Tourist," translated by Darrell B. Lockhart with permission of the author. Originally published in the collection *Amor propio* (Buenos Aires: Alfaguara, 2007).

Julio Cortázar, "Return Trip Tango," from *We Love Glenda So Much and Other Tales* (New York: Knopf, 1984), translated by Gregory Rabassa. English © 1984 Gregory Rabassa. Originally published as "Tango de vuelta" in *Queremos tanto a Glenda* (Madrid: Ediciones Alfaguara, 1980). Reprinted by permission of Random House.

Mempo Giardinelli, "Para toda una eternidad." Originally published in *El castigo de Dios* (Buenos Aires, Argentina: Tesis, Grupo Editorial Norma, 1993) and reprinted in *Cuentos completos* (Argentina: Seix Barral, 1999). Translated by Darrell B. Lockhart from revised edition published in *9 Historias de amor* (2009) with permission of author. Reprinted by permission of Agencia Carmen Balcells, Barcelona.

Luisa Peluffo, "Flechas," has not been previously published. Translated by Beth Pollack by permission of the author. English © 2010 Beth Pollack.

Rodolfo Rabanal. "Letter from Punta del Este," originally published in the journal *Eñe* (No. 6, 2006), Madrid, Editorial La Fábrica as "Carta desde el